Hamlet Himself

Hamlet Himself

Bronson Feldman

iUniverse, Inc.
New York Bloomington

Hamlet Himself

iUniverse books may be ordered through booksellers or by contacting:

iUniverse
1663 Liberty Drive
Bloomington, IN 47403
www.iuniverse.com
1-800-Authors (1-800-288-4677)

Because of the dynamic nature of the Internet, any Web addresses or links contained in this book may have changed since publication and may no longer be valid.

ISBN: 978-1-4502-1185-7 (sc)
ISBN: 978-1-4502-1186-4 (ebk)

Printed in the United States of America

iUniverse rev. date: 2/23/2010

Introduction

[Reprinted from the *Critic and Guide* (Girard, Kansas) vol. 5, no. 6, June 1951]

Nobody knows for sure when the world's greatest magician in literature was born, but old English tradition sets the date of William Shakespeare's birth on St. George's Day, April 23. Now it is not the least odd of the facts that support the claims of Edward de Vere, Earl of Oxford, to the crown of Shakespeare that he was born on April 23, 1550, according to the modern style of calendar. Queen Elizabeth clung to the medieval mode of dating, which makes the Earl's birthday April 12. One thing is certain, in "the uncertain glory of an April day," the boy who became the most mysterious actor on the stage of English public life in the 16th century was born.

We can get a pretty fair idea of what Edward de Vere looked like from the paintings of Will Shakespeare known as the Ashbourne, the Janssen, and the Hampton Court. These were proved by photographic analysis of infra-red rays (reported some years ago by Charles W. Barrell in *Scientific American*) to be portraits of Oxford, concealed for an unknown cause. The Earl's family seems to have regarded him as a black-sheep; one member tried to brand him with the bar sinister of illegitimacy: and not long after his death the church memorial of his grave was allowed to vanish.

When Vere's father, Earl John, died, leaving him as an orphan at 12, he was the proud possessor of more than a hundred estates. His mother, born Margaret Golding, occupied the ancestral castle Hedingham in Essex, but did not stay widow long. She married an obscure knight named Charles Tyrrell, and handed her son over to the care of Sir William Cecil, the Queen's main minister. The resemblance between this family division and the home life of Hamlet is startling. Scholars who reject the Oxford claim to Shakespeare's glory have recognized in Cecil the image of Polonius. Earl Edward married Cecil's daughter Anne, but they did not live happily ever after. The name Tyrrell, by the way, occurs in Richard III, as that of a murderer. It is recorded that Vere's stepfather haunted him with a nightmare whip.

The young earl started life as a courtier with dazzling promise educated in arts and arms, a marvelous horseman, the Queen's favorite in dances, a prodigious writer of love songs. But he wished to be a soldier, or win fame at sea. His father-in-law, when titled Lord Burleigh, did little to advance Vere's ambitions, and jealous clever rivals, like Christopher Hatton and Walter Raleigh, contrived to keep him at home. Once he ran away from the court, like Count Bertram in *All's Well That Ends Well*, to learn the art of war on the continent. But he was forced to return. He came back from the Netherlands with fantastic yarns about his feats of warfare on the Spanish front there, and promotion to a general's staff. These little lies reappeared as literature in *All's Well*. In fury against Burleigh, who had assisted in the execution of Oxford's cousin, the Duke of Norfolk, and in the belief that his wife was unfaithful to him, Vere parted from Countess Anne, like Bertram from his Countess Helena. The Earl fell in love with a dark siren named Anne Vavasor, whose kinsfolk were so outraged by the affair, they provoked a series of street fights with the servants of Oxford. They shed blood in London like the feuding families of Verona in *Romeo and Juliet*. Oxford's Tybalt, or "prince of cats," was Tom Knyvet, the uncle of his love: he nearly wounded Vere to death in a duel. Like the singer of the Sonnets, Oxford was "made lame by fortune's dearest spite." Somehow he and Countess Anne were reconciled. Court rumor claimed it was done by a device exactly like the love-trick in *All's Well* and *Measure for Measure.*

In 1585 Oxford was given the chance to lead English volunteer cavalry in Holland, only to see the chance withdrawn in a few weeks by friends of the Earl of Leicester, his strongest foe at court. Oxford was unlucky in war as in love. When the Spanish Armada sailed into the English Channel in 1588, the Earl hired a ship to encounter the enemy, but missed the great battle at which Admiral Howard and Francis Drake settled the fate of the Atlantic powers. While he was away at the war, his wife died. She left three daughters who all married nobles. The eldest two were apparently unhappy in marriage; one was accused of being false to her husband, Derby: the other's husband, Berkshire, killed himself with an arrow. The youngest girl wedded the Earl of Montgomery, one of the brothers to whom the first edition of Shakespeare's collected plays was dedicated in 1623. *King Lear* swarms with other resemblances to the life of Vere, who is said to have written the tragedy in his last home, Kings's Place. Twelve years before his death he retired from court, and surrendered himself to a kind of underworld existence as companion of players and playwrights. He paid and directed several companies of mummers, and kept poets like Tony Munday, John Lyly, Robin Greene, and Tom Nashe, well supplied with herring and Rhenish wine. Nashe hailed him as "Master William" once, in a letter that was quickly suppressed. As Lord Chamberlain of England, the Earl acted as patron of the troupe that performed Shakespeare's comedies and tragedies. He is known to have tried his hand at drama, and earned a little fame for court comedies which have not survived under his name.

How he lavished away his wealth! He lost 3,000 pounds invested in a deal with the sly Lock, who organized the expedition of Captain Frobisher to find a way to Asia across the New World's northern waters. Surely whoever wrote *The Merchant of Venice* had been banged by the Earl's loss, picturing it in the 3,000 ducat deal with Shylock. What else was Hamlet thinking of when he said he was only "mad north-north-west"? Oxford owed much money to a Jewish banker in Italy, Baptista Spinola, whose name appears barely modified as Baptista Minola—the rich Padua merchant in *The Taming of the Shrew*. And the taming of Katherine the shrew, incidentally, might have been a comedy on the marriage of Oxford's sister Mary, who was celebrated for a tongue like a whiplash. He had a half-sister Katherine who made bitter speeches about the scandals in his life. But Mary's man Peregrine Bertie was a splendid model for Petruchio. Bertie was the brave Lord Willoughby whom the Spaniards extolled as a soldier unafraid of all the devils. He led English volunteers in the war of the Dutch republic, and under his leadership Oxford's country cousins, Francis and Horace Vere, gained the adoration of the English and Dutch troops.

Francis Vere's victories were staged in London by an unknown Company, probably Oxford's, playing at their favorite theater, the Boar's Head inn. Whether this was the same Boar's Head where Falstaff and his crew used to revel is a question not yet determined by the experts. The fighting Veres were dear to the heart of the writing Vere: he tried to leave them the remnants of his fortune, but Burleigh prevented the legacy. After Countess Anne's death, Earl Edward gave up his ambitions of state. He was responsible for the defeat of his political plans because he had sheltered Catholic priests hiding from the royal anger against all those suspected of plotting to crown Catholic May Stuart queen of England. This act of charity was not the last occasion of Oxford's involvement in suspicions of conspiracy against the throne. Even after he married the country heiress Elizabeth Trentham and went to live in suburban tranquility not far from his beloved theaters, there were whispers in the Tower of London that the Earl dreamed of a French invasion that would make young Lord Hastings founder of a new dynasty. But what Oxford was really doing in the last years of his enigmatic life remains in the dark. He delighted in secrecy. From the age of 17, when he had suffered the stigma of a murder-case—killing a servant of Burleigh who had run on his sword, he cloaked himself in mystery.

Evidence for the Oxford claim to the crown of Shakespeare mounts every year. Only a fraction of it is offered here. Captain Bernard Ward's biography of the Earl is a grand pioneer effort to lift the shadows that have hung for centuries over the Vere name. But the most fascinating proof of the claims, first set forth in J. Thomas Looney's *Shakespeare Identified* (1920) and upheld by men like John Galsworthy and Sigmund Freud, will remain in the plays and sonnets of Shakespeare. The 401st anniversary of Vere's birth, this year, takes on poignant meaning to people who have delved into his life and paralleled it with the secret confessions called the comedies and tragedies of William Shakespeare.

I.

From the Sublime

In *The Interpretation of Dreams* Freud responded to the challenge of Shakespeare's Prince of Denmark and tried to "pluck out the heart" of his mystery. He maintained that the peculiar malady of Hamlet—which he diagnosed as a kind of hysteria—had its roots in the filial complex, named by the father of analytic psychology after Oedipus, the legendary Greek king who fulfilled its two criminal desires, getting rid of his father and sleeping with his mother, desires which in children, especially a lad like Hamlet, change to unconscious distorted dreams.

In search of biographic evidence for this view Freud found and copied a statement made by Georg Brandes in his volume on Shakespeare, that the tragedy had taken shape in the poet's imagination soon after the death of his father. This momentous event, perhaps the most important in Shakespeare's whole life, occurred, according to Brandes, a day or two before September 8, 1601, when John Shakspere of Stratford-on-Avon was buried at the town church, no doubt in the presence of William, his famous son. When Freud reviewed the matter not long after 1920, under the influence of *Shakespeare Identified* by J. Thomas Looney, he came to the conclusion that Brandes had misled him, and he repudiated the suggestion that *Hamlet* was composed "under the immediate impact" of the dramatist's bereavement. In a note to the 1930 edition of his work on dreams Freud announced: "I have in the meantime ceased to believe that the author of Shakespeare's works was the man from Stratford."[1] He considered this disbelief enlightening enough to repeat several times in other books.

Freud's loss of faith in the official doctrine concerning the author of Hamlet impressed very few of his followers. (An outstanding exception was Ruth Mack Brunswick, but she did not publish anything on the fact.) Ernest Jones, who elaborated Freud's ideas on the drama in an influential monograph, does not seem to have considered his master's change of view deserving of remark—until he came to write the second volume of his biography of Freud (1955). In *Hamlet and Oedipus* Jones asserted that the customary dates proposed for the Shakespeare canon "go to confirm Freud's suggestion" that it was conceived in the autumn of 1601. But Jones omitted a notice to his readers that this suggestion had been made in 1900 and dropt before 1930 in favor of an extremely different theory.

Freud presented his new conception in the *Outline of Psychoanalysis* which was published after his death. Here he declared: "The name William Shakespeare is very probably a pseudonym, behind which a great unknown concealed himself. One man in whom we believe we recognize the author of the poetical works by Shakespeare, Edward de Vere, Earl of Oxford, lost while still a boy a beloved and admired father, and completely separated from his mother, who contracted a new marriage very soon after the death of her husband."[2]

Ernest Jones rejected the notion that the Prince of Denmark represented a dramatic self-portrait of the Earl of Oxford. He mentions it in a footnote of his monograph, referring to De Vere as one "whom post-Baconians have apparently adopted as their last hope."[3] Now the fact that persons who once adhered to the Baconian theory of Shakespeare-authorship have since been converted to the Oxford theory affords no help at all to answering the question of Hamlet's real identity. It is indeed regrettable that Jones should thus have missed the chance to examine Freud's opinion on the question and the literature that upholds Looney's theory. The examination would not have required half the space that Jones devoted to the notion that Shakespeare had embodied in *Hamlet* a passion for the extravagant lady Mary Fitton—an academic fantasy without a single fact to support it.

The implications of the Brandes-Jones conception of the writing of *Hamlet* merit a study by observers of the irrational in literature and life. According to this conception, the play was composed and produced between September 9, 1601 (the funeral of John Shakspere) and July 26, 1602, when the licensing of *Hamlet* for publication was recorded in the London Stationers' Register. In that interval of less than eleven months John Shakspere's son took care of an inheritance of two houses in Stratford, renting part of one property to a Lewis Hiccocks and another to Joan Hart, his sister, who had married a hatter. William also arranged for the domestic security of his widowed mother and returned to his theatrical business in London and the provinces. He took part in the rehearsal and performance of innumerable plays they gorgeously staged at the royal court during the Christmas holidays of 1601-02. In March 1602 his application for a coat of arms was branded fraudulent by the herald Ralph Brooke. Nevertheless William persevered in his efforts to obtain the honor. We do not know what wires of state were pulled to get it. With the profits from his shares in the Chamberlain's troop, and other rewards of his enterprises, Shakspere purchased in May 1602 a hundred and seven acres of farmland near his home town. Lewis Hiccocks was a tenant on this farm. Since William was too busy to negotiate in person, his brother Gilbert, a haberdasher in London, took charge of the deal. At the same time William contemplated the extension of his holdings of Stratford real estate. He bought twenty acres of pasture for his farm, set a fruit orchard by New Place, his grand house in Stratford, and in September bought a cottage and garden in Dead Lane across the road from his house. While he engaged in these details—we are invited to believe—*Hamlet* was not only written; it had been acted in London, at the universities of Oxford and Cambridge, and also toured the provincial towns. It became so popular on the stage that it was prepared for the press, in shortened form, by an unknown theatrical hand, which prompted the true author to have it printed at full length the next year. Including the satirical remarks of the hero on gentry who ardently acquired real estate and so became "spacious in dirt." According to the Brandes-Jones opinion, this masterpiece, Shakespeare's most personal play, must have been imagined and penned in the midst of countless commercial, histrionic, and family distractions, at a velocity that nobody has yet dared to guess. It is a view which utterly disregards the judgment of Wordsworth and Stendhal that poetry is emotion recollected in tranquility. It also ignores our knowledge of the opposition put up by players in Shakespeare's time to the printing of their plays before they had become rather stale and unprofitable. The demands that Brandes and Jones make on our credulity and common sense are too many and severe. The De Vere theory exacts less from our psychic economy. Let us go over by its light the known facts about *Hamlet* and see where it leads.

A

In the first place, there is proof that the play was well known to the English theater some years before John Shakspere went to his grave. In 1598 an edition of the poetical works of Geffrey Chaucer appeared which the erudite Gabriel Harvey bought. In it he scribbled a praise of Shakespeare and his play: "The younger sort takes much delight in Shakespeare's *Venus and Adonis*: but his Lucrece and his tragedy of *Hamlet, Prince of Denmark* have it in them to please the wiser sort. Or such poets: or better: or none."[4] We have no way of knowing how long after the publication of this Chaucer the note was inscribed. But take the anonymous comedy *Wily Beguiled*, which was almost certainly staged in 1596. It refers to the English expedition to Cadiz in the summer of that year. Among the ludicrous allusions it makes to several of Shakespeare's dramas there is one that points directly to our Danish tragedy. A buffoon speaks of forcing another to "fly swifter than meditation"—a metaphor plainly inspired by Hamlet's phrase, "wings as swift as meditation."[5] In 1596 Thomas Lodge published his *Wit's Misery*, which contains a vivid simile derived from our play: He speaks of a devil so pale he resembled "the vizard of the ghost which cried so miserably at the Theater, like an oyster-wife, 'Hamlet, revenge!'" Two years earlier, on June 8, 1594 the Lord Chamberlain's company, working together with the Lord Admiral's men, performed a tragedy named *Hamlet* in the playhouse at Newington Butts; and the profits from their two hours' work were remarkably small.[6] The Earl of Oxford, by the way, was then living in obscurity in the village of Stoke Newington nearby. By this time, apparently, the tragedy must have been old familiar stuff. In Gabriel Harvey's *New Letter of Notable Contents*, which came out in September 1593, he refers satirically to Hamlet's best known soliloquy. He informs Englishmen who wonder at the piety of certain politicians that the Italian skeptic "Machiavel can teach a Prince to be, and not to be, religious."[7] About the year 1590 there existed a romantic comedy entitled *The Dead Man's Fortune*, of which a plot outline survives. It had a young Greek hero called Laertes. But the name could have been borrowed by the playwright from Homer rather than *Hamlet*. Richard Burbage, who became years afterward illustrious in the role of Hamlet, acted in *The Dead Man's Fortune*. The play is supposed to have belonged to the actors who wore the livery of Ferdinando Stanley, Lord Strange, afterward the Earl of Derby. These actors, prior to 1594, merged with an unknown troop to form the Lord

Chamberlain's company, the company always connected with the name of William Shakespeare.

And now we come to the *Hamlet* to which Thomas Nash alludes in his preface to Robert Greene's novel *Menaphon*, which was registered by the printer on August 23, 1589.

This *Hamlet* of 1589 is the drama that Frederick S. Boas conjectured was written by the little known Thomas Kyd. According to Ernest Jones, the Boas guess has been "strongly confirmed by later research and may now be regarded as almost certainly established."[8] Few investigators who study the evidence for the Kyd claim will share Jones's confidence. It is based entirely on the context of the allusion by Nash.

The paragraph in which Nash refers to our drama is, no doubt, a satire on Kyd, but it clearly distinguishes him from the author of the tragedy. It begins with ridicule of "our trivial translators," in particular "a sort of shifting companions, that run through every art and thrive by none," who had deserted the trade of scrivener, "whereto they were born." Thomas Kyd's father was a scrivener and made his living by copying legal documents. Nash remarks that the deserters of that trade turned to "busy themselves with the endeavors of art," especially dramatic art, although they had only a poor acquaintance with Latin and the classics. "Yet," he continues,

"English Seneca read by candle-light yields many good sentences, as Blood is a Beggar, and so forth. And if you entreat him fair in a frosty morning, he will afford you whole Hamlets, I should say handfuls of tragical speeches. But O grief! Tempus edax rerum: what's that will last always? The sea exhaled by drops will in continuance be dry, and Seneca let blood line by line and page by page at length must needs die to our stage. Which makes his famisht followers to imitate the Kid in Esop, who enamored with the Fox's new-fangles, forsook all hopes of life to leap into a new occupation; and these men, renouncing all possibilities of credit or estimation, to intermeddle with Italian translations."[9]

The pun on Kyd's name is unmistakable. And we know that when Nash wrote these sarcastic lines Kyd had recently published a translation of *Torquato Tasso, The Householder's Philosophy*—registered at Stationers' Hall on February 6, 1588. This means that Kyd had presumably abandoned his occupation with the endeavors of dramatic art prior to February 1588. Why? Because a certain dramatic poet, named by Nash after Seneca, the chief of Latin tragedians, seems to have run dry and "died" so far as the London stage was concerned. (It will be remembered that the poet Edmund Spenser, in *The Tears of the Muses*, composed early in 1590, expressed his sorrow that "Our pleasant Willy, ah! is dead of late," or rather he "doth choose to sit in idle cell...") Whoever this "English Seneca" was, there can be no question that Nash believed the ex-scrivener was deeply obliged to him in the days when he tried to be a dramatist. From this tragic poet, and not from any of the English translations of Roman tragedy, Kyd had copied striking sentences such as "Blood is a beggar." The dramas of this native Seneca, Nash declares, had been studied by Kyd late at night. And the poet himself appears to have given generously of his work when appealed to personally early on a winter day. He still had power, in the summer of 1589, to provide plenty of tragic speeches, indeed "whole Hamlets." However, his followers were hungry and seeking new modes of literary livelihood.

We need not survey here the question of Kyd's own experiments with art and blank verse. It is enough for us to recognize that Thomas Nash knew better than to credit him with the creation of The Prince of Denmark. Perhaps Nash knew or cleverly guessed who did create the noble Dane. "More than one deft phrase," says Grosart in his comment on Nash's satire, "seems inevitably to show that the audacious young rascal had Shakespeare in mind."[10] After a scrutiny of Nash's testimony and chronicles about Hamlet down to 1604, Marshall Evans declared, "If this older *Hamlet* was not

Shakespeare's work, then Shakespeare must have committed a shameless and glaring plagiarism, a thing scarcely done by any of his contemporaries. His unknown forerunner was in truth one of the greatest poets."[11] Cairncross, on the other hand, a scholar thoroly conversant with Boas's arguments and the ensuing research, came to the conclusion that none but Shakespeare of the *Hamlet* we are familiar with could have produced the tragedy to which Thomas Nash alludes.[12]

In short, William Shakespeare was the "English Seneca," just as the classical critic Francis Meres proclaimed him in his *Wit's Treasury* in 1598.

Cairncross dates the writing of the tragedy early in 1589. But he offers us no reason why Shakespeare should have been concerned with the story and theme of the Prince of Denmark at that time. As Nash indicates, the play must have been composed and staged some while before the winter of 1587-88 when the "English Seneca" apparently lost his fertility and Kyd his follower had to busy himself with Tasso's prose. I think we can establish with grateful accuracy the time in which the drama shaped itself in Shakespeare's imagination.

B

The French critic Courdaveaux saw in the image of Hamlet the Dane "the flower of the courtiers of Queen Elizabeth, with all the intellectual culture of the sixteenth century."[13] Many critics have held the same view; yet only an armful ever searched the court of the Queen for a noble individual who suffered from the same perplexity as Shakespeare's prince. Naturally there walked no man who suffered from the identical dilemma: that occurred nowhere but in Shakespeare's fantasy. There lived, however, a courtier, having the richest intellectual culture of Europe, who experienced a problem so like Hamlet's that fellow victims of the filial complex should not have missed him.

As Freud pointed out, there was a poet of Elizabeth's court whose father had died when he was still a child, and whose mother had married again while the funeral bell still echoed in the son's ears. We shall examine the facts and then see what events in the dramatist's manhood prior to the composition of Hamlet revived the desires, the griefs and fantasies of those days when Edward de Vere became an orphan.

John de Vere, the sixteenth Earl of Oxford, died on Monday, August 3, 1562, in his castle of Hedingham in Essex. He was in the prime of life, only 43 years old. Yet he had made his last will and testament just six days before his death. His final sickness and passing must have shocked his little son, the Viscount Bulbeck, profoundly. In the beginning of July he had felt well and happy enough to sign a covenant with the Earl of Huntingdon promising the marriage of his Edward to one of Huntingdon's daughters, Elizabeth or Mary Hastings, within a month after his heir reached the age of eighteen. On June 28 Earl John had accompanied his juggler, his flutist, and troop of stage-players in the city of Ipswich, twenty miles northeast of Hedingham. One week earlier he had busied himself obeying a request of Queen Elizabeth to get ready to meet Mary Stuart, the new Queen of Scotland. Mary did not come, but the pleasure that Lord John derived from his preparations was surely greater than the disappointment. He delighted like a boy in castle revels, forest sports, country games, and theatricals. On April 12 he had celebrated with customary joy and circumstance the twelfth birthday of his only son, and August 5, 1562 would have marked the Earl's fourteenth wedding anniversary.

For 22 days the dead noble lay in his castle while hundreds of servants, tenants and friends came to sorrow and encourage the widow and her two orphans. Then, according to one account, "this John Vere...was buried on Tuesday the 25 of August," at the church of St. Nicholas in the village of Hedingham. A contemporary diary gives a different date: "On the 31st of August was buried in Essex the good Earl," with pomp of heraldry and much mortuary ritual; "and great moan made for him."[14]

Early in the afternoon of September 3, says the same diary, "came riding out of Essex from (the funeral) of the Earl of Oxford his father the young Earl of Oxford," with 140 men on horseback in his company dressed in black. They rode thru London town to Westminster, to the mansion of Sir William Cecil, who acted together with Sir Nicholas Bacon as executor of Lord John's will. Here the orphan Earl was given a new residence. It was his second bereavement in a month. His father had kindly designated the boy one of the executors of his will, but Edward was probably not consulted about this departure from his mother and home. Perhaps Queen Elizabeth herself, more likely the providential Cecil, her Secretary, decided to make him a ward of the state, in the care of Cecil who had recently been appointed Master of the royal wards. The Countess Margery Golding de Vere, however, seems to have been quite willing to see her son leave the castle where he was born, and which he had never left except for a term or two in Queen's College, Cambridge, where he was enrolled, in November 1558, at the age of eight.

Soon after his thirteenth birthday, Edward's guardian received a letter from his mother asking to be set free from the financial obligations of her late husband's estate. The widow saw no reason why she should be held accountable for "those things which, in my Lord's lifetime, were kept most secret from me. And since that time," she protested, "the doubtful declaration of my Lord's debts have so uncertainly fallen out that I had rather leave up the whole doings thereof to my son." With a strange bitterness she told Cecil, "my son, who is under your charge," could have all "the honor or gain (if any be)" from his father's testament.[15] In a law-suit for protection of her title by purchase of the land of Lawshall manor in Suffolk, her name appears as "Margaret Golding, widow."[16] She had taken back her maiden name, most likely in order to marry again.

The exact date of her second marriage is unknown, but it must have taken place soon after she washed her hands of the Oxford debts in April 1563. The man of her choice was Charles Tyrrell, a gentleman so obscure that Burke's standard list of extinct baronetcies calls him Christopher. He was the sixth and youngest son of Sir Thomas Tyrrell, a knight well known in the shire. "As the De Veres," says one historian, "were the representative family of the nobility of Essex, so the Tyrrells may be regarded as the representatives of the knightly families."[17] You can imagine, nevertheless, what the young Earl of Oxford thought of his mother's taking a second husband, from folks inferior to his father, indeed from a family whose blood, in medieval minds, was tinctured by the guilt of half-legendary crimes. English chroniclers taught that one of the Tyrrell ancestors killed William II, son of the Conqueror. Another Tyrrell, they alleged, murdered the boy King Edward V. The man who took lord John de Vere's place at Castle Hedingham was forever a stranger to his stepson. In the unconscious, which might better be termed oblivion, stranger and enemy are synonyms.

It appears that young Oxford, or probably Sir William Cecil sent Charles Tyrrell a fine horse for a wedding present, which was returned to the Earl by his stepfather's own last will. Cecil knew the gentleman's fondness for horses. Tyrrell first appears in the government records as the Master of the Horse in the retinue of John Dudley, Duke of Northumberland. After the fall of Dudley from supreme power in 1553, Charles joined the retinue of Lord Richard Rich of Essex, who recommended him for enlistment among Queen Mary Tudor's gentlemen at arms. Rich wrote to the Queen that Charles Tyrrell wished to serve her and would be furnished with some of his Lordship's own armor.[18] The next record of the gentleman seems to be a letter by the Privy Council of Queen Elizabeth to Edward

Carne, Queen Mary's representative in Rome, instructing him to stop his action in case of disputed matrimony which had been submitted in consequence of a suit by Charles Tyrrell to the Court of the Pope. Tyrrell wanted to annul the marriage of a certain Richard Chetwood and Agnes Woodhull. In order to sunder them he had appealed successfully to Cardinal Pole, the Pope's legate in England, who brought the case in 1558 into the Consistory of St. Paul's Cathedral. The cathedral judges reached an opinion against Chetwood and his wife. They appealed to the mother-church of Rome.[19] I have not been able to ascertain the outcome. My next record of the ungallant if godly Charles presents him as the husband of Margaret Golding, widow, and master of the Earl of Oxford's birthplace. He resided there childless until her death on December 2, 1568. His encounter with the stepson at her funeral was of course a polite solemnity and left no trace for biography. Little more than a year later, in the spring of 1570, Tyrrell died.

We have but a single document of the impression that he made on young De Vere. The Earl once remarked to a drinking companion that his mother's second husband had visited him in the figure of a ghost—"with a whip, which had made a better show in the hand of a carman than of hobgoblin."[20] Does not this joking abut the ghost recall the nervous frivolity of Hamlet following the encounter with his father's fantom? "Ah ha, boy! say'st thou so? Art thou there, true-penny?...you hear this fellow in the cellarage...Well said, old mole! Can'st work i' the earth so fast?" (Act I, Scene 5) Before the Ghost begins talking the prince wonders if it is not a "goblin damn'd."

The mockery with which Shakespeare treats the paternal ghost seems almost reverence by comparison with the disdain he shows for the one live father in his play. Lord Chamberlain Polonius is the only character in the tragedy whose identity may be considered securely determined by the consensus of critics and historians. "In his proper person," Froude stated in 1865,

"Polonius burlesqued Sir William Cecil." The latest biographer of Cecil, Conyers Read, confirms the opinion of Froude. An eminent editor of Shakespeare, Dover Wilson, observes that "the figure of Polonius is almost without doubt intended as a caricature of Burleigh." (Cecil preferred to spell the title of his barony "Burghley.")[21] Unfortunately these authors have left us in the dark about their reflections on the inferences to be drawn from this equation between Burghley and Polonius. For example, they have not informed us of their thoughts on the fact that Shakespeare's hero not only deals contemptuously with his reincarnation of Elizabeth's chief minister: he murders him—and so drives his daughter mad, and afterward slays his son. One would think that the dramatist got a deep sadistic satisfaction from imagining the extinction, in blood, of the Cecil family. Hold on, my learned readers will object: none of your authorities who recognize Burghley in Polonius ever said they saw the former's children in Ophelia and Laertes. True, but that does not mean they did not perceive the likeness. The facts that establish it were available to them all. George Russell French pointed out the resemblance as early as 1869, in his *Shakespeareana Genealogica.* What made them isolate the image of Polonius-Cecil from his family was the terrific implication of the poet's personal hatred toward that house. It cannot be explained at all unless we discern in the figure of Prince Hamlet that "flower of the courtiers of Queen Elizabeth," Edward de Vere.

The Earl's acquaintance with the man who became his father-in-law began in early childhood, for William Cecil was an old friend of his father. In July 1561 Cecil used Lord John's dinner table at Oxford House in London for an important conference with the Privy Council and advocates for the Queen of Scots. Then on August 14 the Queen of England and her secretary Cecil became the Earl's guests at Castle Hedingham and stayed there merrily for five days. Anyone who has observed the eyes of Edward De Vere in his extant portraits (including those which were long reputed to be portraits of William Shakespeare) will apprehend with what precocious fervor the eleven-year-old Viscount Bulbeck watched the features and the behavior of her Majesty—who was then a radiant lady approaching 28—and her infinitely crafty secretary.

Sir William's humor that season was a little soured by his worries over the education of his eldest son. Thomas Cecil had gone to France in May 1561 with his tutor Thomas Windebank, but instead of applying himself to the studies ordained by his father, he was wantonly enjoying himself. On August 17 the angry father dispatched from Castle Hedingham a warning to "Philoponus" (so Windebank was called in their correspondence) that the tutor would be held strictly responsible for the idling of young "Theophilus" in Paris. Sir William described his son's activities in the French capital thus: "Slothfulness in keeping his bed, negligent and rash in expenses, careless in his apparel, an immoderate lover of dice and cards; in study soon weary, in game never." Later he expressed a fear that Thomas would come home "like a spending sot, meet to keep a tennis court." When he heard of the boy's interest in horsemanship, he complained, "I sent him not thither to ride abroad." At Christmas he wrote to the disappointing Tom that he was tired of hearing about his lax conduct and waste of time. Children, he said, as gifts of God ought to be a comfort to their parents but Thomas was the contrary. It is impossible to read these laments and reports of young Cecil's doings as a student in Paris without remembrance of Polonius's lecture to Laertes and the scene in *Hamlet* where he puts a spy on his son's Parisian affairs. Undoubtedly Sir William had his agents in Paris inform him repletely of Tom's life. Thus he learnt that his son's primrose path led him not merely to being a borrower but also an invader of Windebank's money box. Nicholas Throgmorton, the English ambassador, told the harassed father that Tom trifled with a girl who lived near Paris: "She is a maid, and her friends will hardly bear the violating of her." So grieved was Sir William by this news that he wrote to the tutor, he would rather lose his son by an honest death than be troubled with him in this way. He wished that Throgmorton "would commit him secretly to some sharp prison." Finally in May 1562 Thomas sent his father a properly filial letter, entreating him not to be angry any more on account of the "vanities of love" which had consumed his son's time in France. Thomas asked for Sir William's blessing and promised better obedience in the future.[22] The young man kept his word: he grew to be a good soldier, and Elizabeth and his father cheerfully entrusted him with the governorship of a military town. Who else but a dramatist intimate with the Cecils, father and son, could have composed the passages of *Hamlet* that reveal the domestic anxieties of Polonius? Who else but Oxford-Shakespeare could have drawn the old statesman's discussion with his spy about his boy's wildness abroad?—"gaming...drinking, fencing, swearing, quarrelling, drabbing..." Even the picture of Laertes "falling out at tennis" (Act II, Scene 2) emerges from the glimpse we have of Thomas Cecil's passion for the tennis court. Laertes' particular interest in French horsemanship (Act IV, Scene 7) also fits into our home-disclosure of young Tom.

From September 1562 until the spring of 1571 the young Earl of Oxford was an intimate member of Cecil's household. No intellect in England knew Lord Burghley and his kin's ways so well.

If Polonius stands in the drama for Burghley, and his son Laertes reincarnates Thomas, Burghley's son, then we may sensibly expect to find that the nymph Ophelia was created in the image of Burghley's daughter Anne. She loved and married Oxford and lived unhappily ever after. He accused his wife of being devoted to her father, not her husband.[23] Indeed it is Ophelia's loss of her father, not the loss of Hamlet's love, that plunges her to insanity. The poor Countess Anne de Vere did not go mad but she spent nearly all of her married life in tears, worry and despair. She brought all the troubles of her heart to her father. Her Hamlet could not convince her to enter a nunnery; instead, for his sake, she lived for years in the gloomiest of chaste solitudes, virtually divorced.

The fact is that De Vere projected onto his father-in-law the deeply hidden hate he had felt in childhood for his real father, and never had the nerve or the chance to vent on his stepfather. Hamlet murders Polonius in a fury of exultation—with a curtain between them. He cannot speak a clear frank word to his face, nor to his stepfather's until they stand in the reach of death. He talks to them exclusively in riddles and ironies, distilling from his make-believe duels of wits a bliss of superiority that almost blinds him to his actual cowardice. So fearful was his prototype, the dramatist, of confronting the paternal image of his conscience in any living man. Hamlet betrays this terror in the harangue to his mother (Act III, Scene 4) where he calls attention to only one aspect of his father's personality: "An eye like Mars', to threaten and command."

Hamlet's hostility to Polonius reminds me of the ambiguity with which Barnaby Fitzpatrick once praised Sir William Cecil. "You make me think the care you take for me," the duly grateful Fitzpatrick wrote, "more fatherly than friendly."[24]

Between the two quarto editions of *Hamlet* Shakespeare changed the name of the Lord Chamberlain of Denmark, from Corambis to Polonius. Percy Allen (a "post-Baconian") has remarked that the word Corambis conveys a joke at William Cecil's expense.[25] The statesman's motto was "Cor unum, via una." Our dramatist did not consider the great man so singularly monotonous. He nicknamed him "double-heart." That was not an injustice to the peerless politician, who had served at one time both the Duke of Somerset and his enemy the Duke of Northumberland, and who showed more than lip-loyalty to the latter and his pawn-queen Jane Grey in the very hours when he, Cecil, was striving to convince Queen Mary Tudor that he was hers to command in body and mind.

Cecil had even contrived to sustain a Protestant heart while faithfully attending the Catholic mass and manifesting a modest adoration for the rosary and the cross. For such agility of soul the plebeian Burghley's patrician son-in-law was bound to feel a grandiose disdain! The stage name Corambis fitted Cecil like a glove also for the good reason that the Master of the Court of Wards rejoiced in his expert management of the writ of Coram Nobis issued for minors or persons deprived of rights while accused of lunacy.

The Earl himself was a peerless artist in hypocrisy, and in one of his Hamlet moods would admit that he was "indifferent honest" and not to be taken at his word. Hamlet confesses to Ophelia that he has performed nameless crimes: "I could accuse me of such things that it were better my mother had not borne me" (Act III, Scene 1). If Edward de Vere had indeed been guilty of the things with which his enemies charged him, he would have attained the eminence of the greatest monster in the history of literature. They accused him of blasphemy, witchcraft, pederastic cruelties, plotting and instigating a variety of murders, and treason, too. The worst that Hamlet can cay about his sins is: "I am very proud, revengeful, ambitious..." He will not acknowledge his vice of jealousy, which spurs him to vengeance on the father who deprived him of Ophelia and the king who usurped the place he coveted in his mother's heart. "For," as the Queen in the first quarto of *Hamlet* observes, "murderous minds are always jealous."

Shakespeare named the Queen, the object of the prince's jealousy, Gertrude. The Danish historian Saxo Grammaticus and the French storyteller Francois de Belleforest, from whose *Histoires Tragiques* our poet obtained the tale of Hamlet, call his mother Geruth. Possibly this recalled to the Earl of Oxford the last two syllables of his own mother's name. Thinking of the widow Margaret might have made him miserable with the word Geruth. The poet's variation was perhaps inspired by the fact that the name Gertrude was a favorite of the Tyrrell family. In the chronicles of Essex one of the Gertrude Tyrrells is particularly noted as a niece of Oxford's stepfather, but why, we are not told.

Another character in *Hamlet* whose name may be traced to the years preceding De Vere's puberty is the prince's friend Guildenstern. When Viscount Bulbeck was nine years old, the Swedish ambassador Nils Guildenstern voyaged to England to persuade the Queen to marry his crown prince Eric. In London he found an ambassador from Denmark, secretly engaged in a scheme for an alliance marital and military between Elizabeth and King Frederick II. October 1559 offered Edward de Vere a chance to meet a Baltic princeling in the flesh, Duke John of Finland, the King of Sweden's second son. John sailed into Essex on his way to woo the Queen for his brother's sake. On the morning of October 1 Earl John de Vere welcomed the Duke and appointed Sir Thomas Smith, his son's excellent teacher, to converse with him. The Duke, the Earl and Sir Thomas, with their host of comrades, enjoyed themselves hugely. In Oxford's company, Smith wrote to Cecil, the Swede soon learnt "to leave off his high looks and pontificality." In the same letter Sir Thomas delivered some cordial remarks about the popularity of his pupil's father: "the love that the gentlemen and the whole country bear to him, whether for the antiquity of his ancestry, or his own gentleness, or the dexterity of these that are about (him), or rather all these." The Duke was conducted from the port of Colchester to the capital by Earl John and Lord Robert Dudley, son of the fallen Duke of Northumberland; young Dudley was now the Master of the Queen's cavalry. Before and after them rode a great number of gentlemen, including eighty who wore the tawny livery of De Vere, with gold chains around their necks, followed by two hundred tall yeomen, half of whom displayed the same livery, all having the Earl's emblem of the blue boar embroidered on the left shoulder. They rode to Oxford House in Candlewick Street, by the historic London Stone. Here was a pageant to stir the pulse of any boy, especially a boy in love with ancient history and contemporary theater, already a student in Cambridge University. During the Christmas holidays Earl John entertained the Duke of Finland with the sport of hawking and hunting in the valley of the Stour. On this occasion Viscount Bulbeck may have met the Swedish ambassador Guildenstern.[26]

He surely could have heard in those days about the clan of the Rosencrantzes. A Dane named Georgius Rossenkrantz signed a letter to Queen Elizabeth in the summer of 1588 from the Senate of Denmark extolling the old friendship of their kingdoms. The quaint name may have reminded Edward de Vere of a tavern called the Rose and Crown. There was an old inn with this name close to Sudbury church, not far from Castle Hedingham, when Havelock Ellis came to live in East Anglis.[26a]

Sir Thomas Smith was not a man to let pass so golden an opportunity as the arrival of the prince of Finland for a lecture to young Edward on the relations of the English with the Swedes and the Danes. His own mind, I imagine, throbbed in October 1559 with the excitement of Baltic history which was still news. On January 24 Christian the Fiery died in his lost kingdom of Denmark, in prison and partially insane. This was the monarch who had outraged his barons and burgesses by assailing their feudal privileges and strengthening the concerns of peasants, artisans and mariners. In his struggle with the lords of church and state, he encountered a weapon of fatal effect in their charge that he was a libertine, worse than any bloody, bawdy villain in the Catholic South. The damned Christian with the title of "the Nero of the North." An armed uprising in alliance with the merchants of Lubeck and their Hansa League drove him out of Denmark and he fled with his family to Spanish protection in the Netherlands. The Danish nobles elected his uncle Frederik king. The fiery nephew dared to return from exile and was captured and locked behind bars, where he finally died, half-crazed. With this tragedy for text, the charming Smith, who believed in astrology and predestination, could have spun many lessons for Oxford's heir.

C

Some months after the orphan Earl's arrival at Cecil House in Westminster, his guardian became warmly interested in the promotion of English naval industry. Cecil was disturbed by the impoverishment of English trade with Ireland which ensued when the King of Denmark regained the dominion of Ireland. The Dane had also demanded higher tolls from English merchants entering the Baltic Sea. By February 1563 Cecil ripened his plan for increasing the native navigation by legally stimulating the English fisheries. He wrote a series of "Arguments to prove that it is necessary for the restoring of the navy of England to have more fish eaten." His proposal, soon adopted as a royal decree, made every Wednesday a day for compulsory eating of fish instead of meat.[27] I suggest that here we may discover the reason why Hamlet, assuring Polonius that he knows him excellent well, declares: "You are a fishmonger."

The man who created this Chamberlain of Denmark was more than familiar with the details of Burghley's career. He had mastered the individual language of his Lordship. The style is the statesman. Shakespeare certainly lingered many times over the peculiar combination of garrulity and reticence by which the Lord Treasurer of England exprest himself. For Nicholas Bacon, in July 1563, blamed Cecil in vain for not loving plain dealing and being too fond of repetitious talk. Cecil chose to take his crony's words as a criticism of his wits, and replied: "I assure you, my Lord, what weakness soever you find in my understanding, you shall find me in that quarrel no baby, nor one that will learn of you more than I have."[28] This denial of babyish behavior reminds me of Hamlet's derision of Polonius: "that great baby you see there is not yet out of his swaddling clouts" (Act II, Scene 2). Burghley's occasional affectation of an imp-like and naïve manner did not always amuse his colleagues and wards. His cunning in language was well described by the Scottish diplomat Maitland: "I have ever found that fault with you," he wrote to De Vere's guardian in August 1563, "that as in your letters you always wrote obscurely, in private communication you seldom uttered your own judgment...you walk so warily, observing rather to speak nothing may any time thereafter hurt yourself than to speak all things might further the matter."[29] Only a close daily association with the old man could have enabled Shakespeare to catch so perfectly his every cadence of tongue and render it with the right matter and art from the mask of Polonius.

Young De Vere pursued his academic studies to the degree of Master of Arts in August 1564. He attended St John's College in Cambridge, the same school that Cecil had attended without getting a degree. The university encouraged its pupils to practice histrionics in Greek and Latin plays, both classical and modern. We know that William Cecil had a talent for masquerade outside politics, which he displayed, to his own entertainment at least, while a student of law at Gray's Inn. So it is entirely natural for Hamlet to engage Polonius in their little dialog about dramatics thus:

> "My lord, you play'd once i' the university, you say?"
> "That did I, my lord, and was accounted a good actor."
>
> (Act III, Scene 2)

In an earlier scene Polonius remarks, "truly in my youth I suffered much extremity for love" (Act II, Scene 2). It is not easy to conceive this eternally calculating political economist as a passionate youth. But Shakespeare knew how Burghley had been tormented in early manhood when he loved and secretly married Anne Cheke, the daughter of a wineshop keeper in Cambridge, despite his father's opposition. The mother of Thomas Cecil died two years later. When William Cecil married again he selected his bride, Mildred Cooke, with the frigid wisdom for which he won the renown of an English Nestor. Lady Mildred was the mother of Edward de Vere's first wife, and exerted a mighty and sometimes frightening influence in his life, an influence for which the writer of *Hamlet* found no space in his play. He settled one account with his mother-in-law in the romance of *Cymbeline*, which I believe with Eva Turner Clarke, was played first for the Queen under the title "the Cruelty of a Stepmother," on Innocents night, 1578.

As a guardian the political polymath Cecil exhibited no less care for the orphan Earl of Oxford than he showed for his own son, concerning whom he confessed in May 1561: "indeed to this hour I never showed any fatherly fancy to him but in teaching and correcting."[29] Not many months passed before a clandestine spiritual feud began flaring between Earl Edward and Sir William, a mental fight whose conclusion will not be reached until the theater of William Shakespeare dissolves to oblivion.

As a ward of the state little Oxford looked of course to Queen Elizabeth for a maternal treatment. His behavior toward her probably disclosed how he felt and what he unconsciously thought when he lived with the Countess Margaret. He must have become acquainted early with the natural gossip about the Queen's erotic life. All sorts of rumors circulated about her amorous feelings for Lord Robert Dudley, fantasies which provoked a fierce jealousy in the courtiers who rivaled Dudley for her imperial favors. At the head of the court faction that hated Dudley and wished he would die as suddenly and mysteriously as his young and country-refined wife, the late Amy Robsart, had died, stood Thomas Radcliff, Earl of Sussex, and his kinsman Thomas Howard, Duke of Norfolk, the son of

Frances de Vere, Earl Edward's aunt. Allied by blood and ideals with the house of Howard, young Oxford quickly entered the Sussex faction, emboldened by his private envy of the love that Elizabeth showed Lord Robert everywhere. After she elevated her favorite to the earldom of Leycester, his pride became unendurable to the aristocrats of purpler stock. Sussex grieved to the Queen that Leycester disobeyed her command that neither Earl should molest the other, and was assembling bands of armed men to waylay his antagonist. Elizabeth compelled a truce. The feud never came to bloodshed, but it left scars in literature which have not healed yet. It is no accident, for instance, that Georg Brandes associates the Earl of Leycester and Shakespeare's King of Denmark in speaking of alleged criminal secrets of the Tudor Court.[30]

At the age of seventeen Edward de Vere himself became a homicide. Cecil described the event in his diary under the date July 23, 1567: "Tho. Bryncknell, an under-cook, was hurt by the Earl of Oxford at Cecil House in the Strand, whereof he died; and by a verdict found felo de se with running upon a point of a fence sword of the said Earl." Years later Burghley referred to the deed in a list of the benefits he had done for De Vere: "I did my best to have the jury find the death of the poor man whom he killed in my house se defendendo."[31] The jury's own record has not been printed yet. Burghley's two versions of the verdict, beside his failure to state De Vere's view of the affair, plainly indicate that something was rotten in the state of Cecil House in the Strand when Thomas Brinknell died. Looney connects his death with the killing of Polonius and the bitterness of Hamlet over the dead body of that spy: "Thou wretched, rash, intruding fool, farewell! I took thee for thy better." There seems to be an echo of the jury's bewilderment over the manner in which the cook was killed in the passage of *Hamlet* where the gravediggers dispute on the drowning of Ophelia, whether it was accident or suicide. One thing is clear: Oxford's fencing blade, like the foil of Laertes in his fatal bout with Hamlet, was without its safety button when he collided with the poor Tom.

We do not know if the cook's ghost haunted the Earl. But we have the testimony of a courtier familiar with his wine-talk that young De Vere claimed he had often seen the Devil by conjuring; and the vision, by his direction, was painted in a book of prophecies he secretly kept.[32] Unfortunately the book was not preserved. So we are ignorant of the form in which his prophetic soul conceived of the Prince of Darkness.

"The Devil hath power," Hamlet fancies, "To assume a pleasing shape." The martial guise of his father seems to have pleased the prince more than his author would say. Earl Edward's father educated his son to use his life in the service of his country by means of arms and arts, but above all by arms. Lord John himself had little experience of arms in action: he had seen some skirmishes with Henry VIII in France and served at the siege of Boulogne, no more. So potent, however, was the soldierly ideal he upheld to his son that the poet could never bear to believe that he might have failed as a man of war. Perfection of humanity signified for him "The courtier's, soldier's, scholar's eye, tongue, sword." Both in Castle Hedingham and Cecil House the daydreams dearest to him were dreamt in the armory room. He confided his military aspirations to Cecil and pleaded with him to gain the Queen's goodwill to his going overseas in order to learn the skills of battle in a foreign field of blood. Cecil did not take his aspiration seriously; he kept the young man at his books.

In the year of Tom Brinknell's death a ballad (now lost) appeared which may be the one that Hamlet quoted or sang to Polonius. The "Song of Jephthah's Daughter at Her Death" was licensed for printing by Alexander Lacy in 1567. Hamlet calls the Chamberlain by the name of Israel's judge (Act II, Scene 2). He responds, echoing the ballad, "If you call me Jephthah, my lord, I have a daughter that I love passing well." "Nay, that follows not," says the prince punning on the use of the word "follow" in logic and its ordinary sense of coming next. "The first row of the pious chanson will show you more." Judging by fragments of the ballad recorded by Thomas Percy two centuries after, the first stanza apparently went thus:

Have you not heard these many years ago,
Jephthah was judge of Israel?
He had one only daughter and no mo',
The which he loved passing well.
And as by lot,
God wot,
It came to pass,
As god's will was,
That great wars there should be,
And none should be chosen chief but he.

Hamlet varies a couplet: "It came to pass," says he, "As most like it was—" He refused to believe it was God's will that Jephthah-Polonius should be chosen the main minister of his nation in the war crisis brought on by the kingdom of Norway in the play. Shakespeare never forgot the cruelty shown by the Jewish warchief in sacrificing his daughter to keep the vow he had made to God to render up to him the first live thing he met on returning victorious from war. In the tragedy of *Henry VI*, Part Three, the dramatist condemns the chief from the mouth of Clarence, when he rejects the vow of allegiance he had sworn to the house of Lancaster (Act V, Scene 1):

To keep that oath were more impiety
Than Jephthah's when he sacrific'd his daughter.

What Hamlet's Biblical allusion amounts to, then, is an accusation by his creator that William Cecil was the sort of man who would doom his daughter to a tragic end for the sake of a triumph in policy. We shall see, with Cecil himself as a witness, how far this blame was justifiable. Students of Cambridge University, Trinity College, played a lost tragedy called *Jephthes* in this somber year 1567.

The year 1568 saw the publication of a book which would have interested the Earl of Oxford for several strong reasons. It was entitled "A discovery and Plain Declaration of Sundry Subtle Practices of the Holy Inquisition of Spain" by Reginald Montanus. Vincent Skinner of Lincoln's Inn translated it: a gentleman who became one of Cecil's privately trusted secretaries. Skinner's quiet energy in Cecil's service and his work on the "subtle practices" of the Church in Spain probably furnished Shakespeare with the name of the spy whom Polonius set on the path of Laertes in France. In the first quarto of *Hamlet* the spy is called Montano. He enters the second edition changed to Reynaldo. The name Reginald, as in the case of Cardinal Pole, was commonly turned in England to Reynold. In the person of Polonius's agent "Reynaldo-Montano" we have presumably a bare sketch of Burghley's agent, the translator of Reginald Montanus.

In the same year the captive Queen Mary Stewart heard of a subtle game played by the Scottish Earl of Murray and the English Earl of Hertford to see which of the two should marry "one of the Secretary Cecil's daughters." Nothing came of their intrigue; but it would be a wonder if the Secretary did not learn about it from one of his legion of spies.

On December 2, 1568 the Countess Margaret of Oxford, "wife of Charles Tyrrell, Esquire," died at Castle Hedingham. Her only son was surely among the chief mourners at her burial in his ancestral tomb at Earls Colne, where she was placed by the side of his father's corpse. On returning to London he attempted to vanquish his mingled emotions about her by diverting his thoughts to literature. He was especially entranced by the ancient Greek novels that told of parents and lovers separated from their children and each other by various disasters and reunited, after fabulous adventures, in a bliss of love without further history. The first work of fiction dedicated to the Earl of Oxford was one of these romances, the famous *Ethiopian History* by Heliodorus, translated by Thomas Underdowne in 1569. From the dream-like material of these tales Shakespeare contrived the plots of his earliest plays, and to them he returned in his old age.

The reader has probably noticed a curious difference between the ballad of Jephthah as given by Bishop Percy and the song recited by Hamlet. Instead of "He had one only daughter and no mo'," he declaims: "One fair daughter, and no more." The model for Polonius had two daughters, Anne and Elizabeth. Only the elder seems to have won from observers the tribute of a pretty, attractive girl. Her father understood whom Sir Henry Sidney meant when he wrote, in November 1568, his respects to Lady Mildred and "my sweet jewel, your daughter." Two months later Sidney proposed that his son Philip should marry Anne. William Cecil liked Philip Sidney very much—"my darling Philip," he called him—but he judged the Sidneys too poor in this world's goods to make a proper match for his Nan. Nevertheless, for a whole year the thrifty Sir William negotiated with Sir Henry and Philip's uncle, the Earl of Leycester, to learn what economic limits they set to a wedding alliance with him. After considerable bargaining and calculation, a "coldness" emerged between them which Cecil deplored, in February 1570, hindered him from going ahead with the deal. He disliked Leycester, and the royal favorite also did what he could, politely and subtly, to undermine Cecil's power with the Queen. Moreover our Polonius was convinced that his Ophelia was worthy of becoming a bride in a loftier sphere than the Sidneys inhabited. He explored the possibility of nuptials with Gilbert Talbot, the son of the Earl of Shrewsbury, but the Talbots declined the temptation.[33] In February 1571 the Queen promoted Cecil to the barony of Burghley. He protested that he was "the poorest lord in

England," but now he simply could not marry his Anne to anyone less than a lord.

In the spring of 1571 a courtier sent news to young Edward Manners, Earl of Rutland, who had recently ended his period of wardship with Cecil and gone traveling in France. "There is no man," ran the news, "of life and agility in every respect in Court but the Earl of Oxford." In July another courtier informed Rutland that Anne Cecil had succeeded in capturing Oxford; Elizabeth consented to their union, while her Maids of Honor ostentatiously lamented Anne's luck. On August 15 Lord Burghley himself wrote to Rutland about it. With ponderous coyness he hinted that he would have preferred a different Earl for his daughter: "Truly, my Lord, my goodwill served me to have moved such a matter as this in another (direction than this) is, but having some occasion to doubt of the issue of the matter, I did forbear; and in mine own conceit I could have as well liked there as in any other place in England. Percase your lordship may guess where I mean, and so shall I, for I will name nobody.

"Now that the matter is determined betwixt my Lord of Oxford and me, I confess to your Lordship I do honor him so dearly as much as I can any subject, and I love him so dearly from my heart as I do mine own son, and in any case that may touch him for his honor and weal, I shall think mine own interest therein. And surely, my Lord," Burghley added, "by dealing with him I find that which I often heard of your Lordship, that there is much more in him of understanding than any stranger to him would think."[34]

In copying that last remark, a line from the first printed version of *Hamlet* recurred to me, King Claudius's comment on the prince: "There's more in him than shallow eyes can see." Parallel to both opinions may be set the words of Polonius on the surprising sense that Hamlet revealed in the midst of his habitual riddling talk: "How pregnant sometimes his replies are! A happiness that often madness hits on."

The wedding of Earl Edward and Anne took place in Westminster Abbey on December 19, 1571, a fortnight after her fifteenth birthday. Among the guests of course were Thomas Cecil and his wife Dorothy, the daughter of Lord John Latimer, whose mother Dorothy de Vere, was the sister of the fourteenth Earl of Oxford. Perhaps others at the wedding beside Burghley remembered what Sir Henry Percy had said when Thomas Cecil was a bachelor: "I think it were not amiss if he were planted in some stock of honor."[35] Perhaps Shakespeare heard of the saying and had it in mind while writing the dialog of Hamlet and Ophelia concerning marriages. "You should not have believed me" says the prince; "for virtue cannot so inoculate our old stock but we shall relish of it."

After the marriage festivities and the Christmas revels that followed, Oxford received from his friend Thomas Bedingfield a manuscript he had long desired. It was Bedingfield's translation of Girolamo Cardano's *De Consolatione* (1542). *Cardanus' Comfort* was published in 1573 "by commandment of the right honorable the Earl of Oxford," together with a preface and a poem by the Earl. Although this fact has passed without comment by the professors of English literature, they have not stinted praise of the book itself, nor underestimated its importance in the making of *Hamlet.* Some have fancied the *Comfort* to be the very volume that Shakespeare meant his hero to read on the stage. Hardin Craig extols it as "Hamlet's Book."[26] We have only to glance through its pages to recognize how large an influence this Italian philosophy had on our dramatist.

One of the purposes of Cardano in writing it was to relieve his readers of "the sorrow which chanceth by the death of parents." He exhorted orphans to fortify their minds against the woe and terror of death. "What should we account of death to be resembled to anything better than sleep?" Speaking of slumbers, he affirmed, "those are best wherein, like unto dead men, we dream nothing." A dream that Cardano apparently dreaded was one in which he went on a certain journey: there is nothing, he said, "that doth better or more truly prophesy the end of life than when a man dreameth that he doth travel... and that he traveleth in countries unknown without hope of return." But no man should brood over such dreams and prophecies to the point of losing the native hue of his courage. After all, "we are assured not only to sleep, but also to die...to bear everything resolutely is not only the part of a wise man, but also of a man well advised." "Only honesty and virtue of mind," he warned, "doth make a man happy and only a cowardly and corrupt conscience do cause thine unhappiness." All students of *Hamlet* will freely associate these words with the corresponding verses of the play. Nor will they have difficulty now in identifying the source of the Prince's cry, "A beast, that lacks discourse of reason, would have mourn'd longer." According to *Cardanus' Comfort*, "Beasts therefore be able for one only art, by memory, not perceiving reason at any time." From the same cherished authority Shakespeare possibly drew the idea for Hamlet's maxim, "There's nothing either good or bad but thinking makes it so." The Italian or his translator put it more tersely: "A man is nothing but his mind." Ultimately, to be sure, the origin of Hamlet's wisdom is the statement by the Greek skeptic Sextus Empiricus, "our opinion gives the name of good or ill to everything." Our poet, however, did not need any philosopher to tell him, "Old men's company (is) unpleasant." Cardano was very young when he wrote that. Shakespeare, you know, wrote a song on the argument, "Crabbed age and youth cannot live together." The significance of this belief of his for the sorrow "that chanceth by the death of parents," he did not investigate.

There is one statement in *Cardanus' Comfort* that sends a curious light on the old German version of *Hamlet*, which imitated the tragedy as it was staged on the continent by English actors prior to 1602. "The tragical poets," said Cardano, "have found the tragedies and furies to be only in kings' courts." Shakespeare certainly held the Renaissance opinion that tragedy was a form of drama whose characters could not come from a class inferior to nobility. But in none of his extant dramas do we find the Renaissance device of haunting royal courts with the classic Greek furies. The German *Hamlet* opens with a prolog showing the goddess of night, Hecate, summoning the Furies, Alecto, Thisiphone and Megaera, to the court of Denmark. They proclaim that fornication and murder have been committed here and call for revenge. It is conceivable that young Shakespeare provided the original Hamlet with a Senecan scene like this. The appearance of Hecate in the prolog would harmonize with the reference to her, otherwise unnecessary, in the play within the play, where Lucianus gloats over his poison: "With Hecate's ban thrice blasted, thrice infected."

At the time Shakespeare conceived his *Hamlet* the most popular drama of the period, *The Spanish Tragedy*, was still fresh on the stage; and it begins with a convocation of the three furies. Our poet admired that play immensely and may have been tempted, in starting the Danish tragedy, to emulate its Senecan design.

Experts on Tudor dramaturgy have long been acquainted with the likeness between *Hamlet* and the dramas of Greek and Latin antiquity concerning Agamemnon and Merope. Seneca's *Agamemnon* especially, with its opening phenomenon of a tortured ghost, its queen guilty of adultery, its hero slain after returning victorious from war, and details such as the allusions to weeping Niobe, slaughtered Priam, frenzied Hecuba, gleamed on the threshold of Shakespeare's consciousness when he worked on his masterpiece. The Roman tragedy gave him his picture of piling earth to overtop Mount Pelion and Olympus, also perhaps the references of Hamlet to "the terrible lion of Nemea" and its conqueror Hercules. Even the initial stage setting of Hamlet may have been inspired by the vision in the Agamemnon of a crag frowning over the sea, against which the hero's ship was wrecked. The "fateful madness" of the hero's son, avenging the murder of his father, is certainly paralleled by the mock-madness of the Prince of Denmark. And it is not unlikely that the prince's contrast of his two kings, when he upbraids his mother, owes something to Seneca's heroine's lines:

> Dost think that I would leave a king of kings
> And stoop to wed an outcast wretch like thee?

While the manuscript of *Cardanus' Comfort*, early in 1572, lay secluded among De Vere's literary treasures—"murdered," in his phrase, "in the waste bottom of my chests"—his first cousin, the Duke of Norfolk was condemned to death for conspiring to marry Queen Mary Stuart and set her on England's throne. The Earl exerted all his powers to rescue, to win a pardon for the Duke. Elizabeth signed the death warrant with extreme reluctance and withheld it for five months. Finally, on June 2, Howard went to the execution block. He was 36 years old. His cousin of Oxford became frantic with hate of Leycester and Burghley for their desire of Norfolk's destruction, and he swore that he would get revenge. Exercising his genius for histrionics, he dissembled his hate. He wrote to his father-in-law in September warning him to beware of assassins from the camp of the Papacy or Norfolk's numerous friends. Burghley heard that the English Papists in the Low Countries were rejoicing over rumors that the Earl had parted from his wife. Other "sinister reports" made the statesman suspicious of his son-in-law; he proceeded to act as if Oxford was a foe. A letter by De Vere late in October alluded to "so many storms" he had endured from Cecil's "heavy grace" toward him. It makes no mention of the trivial tactics he employed to embitter his Countess' life. In his suppressed fury he went so far as to engage in secret conversations with agents of Spain and the Queen of Scots.[37]

What encouraged the Earl to behave in this way was the Queen's enjoyment of his talents and charms. "My Lord of Oxford," wrote Gilbert Talbot in May 1573, "is lately grown into great credit; for the Queen's Majesty delighteth more in his personage and his dancing and valiantness than any other…I think Sussex doth back him all that he can. If it were not for his fickle head, he would pass any of them shortly. My Lady Burghley unwisely hath declared herself, as it were, jealous, which is come to the Queen's ear; whereat she hath been not a little offended with her, but now she is reconciled again. At all these love matters my Lord Treasurer winketh, and will not meddle in any way."[38] Elizabeth's quasiamorous behavior toward De Vere—her stimulating of his fantasies of royal passion and promotion—heartened him to impudence, rebellion against the Lord Treasurer, which he found very difficult to control. He strove to be diplomatic and assumed a contrite and subservient manner, ever hoping to gain the elder statesman's support for his claim to a military career. But even if Burghley had been favorable, Oxford's "fickle head" would have contrived the necessary devices to frustrate his conscious aims. He strained her Majesty's generosity to the breaking point. The story of this period as seen by the victim-artist has been told in the play *All's Well That Ends Well.*

Denied an outlet for his energy in education as a soldier, denied permission to see the world beyond the English Channel, young Oxford fretted away his days and nights in a bewildering variety of amusements. He pursued an interest in astrology, in alchemy and magic, the black arts to which he had been introduced in boyhood by Sir Thomas Smith. He paid serious attention to Dr John Dee, who solemnly stated that he could discover buried wealth by means of dreams or the rambling and rhapsodic utterances of persons dwelling near such wealth—"speech formed to their imagination by night."[39] A trace of the spellbinding of Dee's research can be seen in *Hamlet* in the speech of Horatio to the Ghost:

> Or if thou hast uphoarded in thy life
> Extorted treasure in the womb of earth,
> (For which, they say, you spirits oft walk in death)
> Speak of it.

For physical pleasure the Earl usually resorted to horsemanship. His brilliance on horseback excited the poets Giles Fletcher and John Southern to lyrical marveling. In "the Centaurian art," as the Frenchman Southern styled it, Oxford seems to have equalled Monsieur Lamord of Normandy, who is so warmly praised in Hamlet.

In January 1575, after wringing from Burghley with laborsome petition his slow leave, the Earl obtained a royal license to travel abroad for a year. He journeyed thru Germany, stopping in Strasburg for discourse with the great Johannes Sturmius, the rector of Strasburg Academy, who always remembered him with admiration. While in Italy De Vere informed the Lord Treasurer (on January 3, 1576) that he had made "an end of all hope to help myself by her Majesty's service—considering that my youth is objected unto me, and for every step of mine a block is found to be laid in my way." Precisely like Prince Hamlet he complained that he lacked advancement. When Rosencrantz tells the prince that he has the vote of the King for his succession to the crown, Hamlet answers, "Ay, sir, but 'While the grass grows—" The proverb is something musty." The old saying is quoted in the same psychological context by Oxford in his letter to Burghley: "I am to content myself according to the English proverb, that it is my hap to starve while the grass doth grow."

He returned from France in April 1576, determined to lead a bachelor's life again. "Ere we were two days old at sea, a pirate of very warlike appointment gave us chase. Finding ourselves too slow of sail, we put on a compelled valor..." The words are Hamlet's: the adventure happened to De Vere. There were actually three pirate vessels encountered on his voyage from Calais to Dover; they robbed him and let him go on his way.[40]

In 1576 Francois de Belleforest published at Lyons the fifth volume of his *Histoires Tragiques*. (Oxford, by the way, visited Lyons in March.)This volume includes the barbaric legend of Amleth out of which Shakespeare wove his play. The chapter is headed "By what ruse Amleth, who afterward becam King of Dannemarch, avenged the death of his father Horvendille, killed by Fengon his brother, and other events of his history." This Amleth pretends to be lunatic, and when King Fengon orders a nameless girl to lure him into fornication—which would prove the prince was not crazy—he eludes his watchers and enjoys her at leisure. After his coronation he voyages to England where the king attempts to kill him by a stratagem. He kills the Englishman and sails home to Denmark triumphant, bringing two wives. One of these, Hermetrude, betrays him for love of his uncle Wiglerus, who plots the overthrow of Amleth and bloodily succeeds, then weds his nephew's widow. It is my belief that when De Vere first read this crude narrative, he started to think of its potentiality for the theater. In the spring of 1576 he composed his first play, the "History of Error," known to us now as the *Comedy of Errors*, and soon afterward wrote the "History of the Solitary Knight," which I have conjectured is the romance we call *Pericles, Prince of Tyre*.[41] Later Belleforest provided him with the material for *Much Ado About Nothing* and *Romeo and Juliet*.

A much discussed mixing of metaphors in *Hamlet* had a rational basis in a book that came out in 1576, *Aelian's Histories*, translated by Abraham Fleming; it describes the Celtic barbarians of Britain taking up arms exactly as Shakespeare says, against a sea of troubles: "They throw themselves into the foaming floods with their swords drawn in their hands."

In this epochal year 1576 Oxford published some of his poems in *The Paradise of Dainty Devices*, poems in no way inferior, I am sure, to the songs Hamlet is said to have made for Ophelia, the lyric Polonius found beginning "Doubt thou the stars are fire," or the dozen or sixteen verses the prince inserted in the little tragedy *The Murder of Gonzago*. The story of that tragedy, Hamlet tells us, "is extant, and writ in very choice Italian." The poet may have seen it in Italy. When the Earl visited Mantua his passion for the princely woes of history would not have overlooked the drama of Luigi Gonzaga, who in 1538 assassinated Francesco della Rovere, the Duke of Urbino by pouring a venomous lotion into his ear. The Duke's wife belonged to the Gonzaga kin—she was the sister of the Duke of Mantua—and Luigi may have been prompted to the murder by incestuous love for her. The similarity of Luigi and Lucianus, the villain of Hamlet's little play, extends no further. Why Shakespeare should have placed the crime of Lucianus in the city of Vienna remains a mystery. The fact that he had recently, in *Measure for Measure*, set the scene of an adventure of another Gonzaga, Vincentio, in that metropolis had something to do with it.

In September 1576 the physician and philosopher Girolamo Cardano died in Rome. On learning the news the Earl of Oxford must have felt that he had lost a distant counselor. He felt the need of a second printing of *Cardanus' Comfort* this year.

His melancholy was relieved the next summer by the warmth of admiration that developed between his sister Mary and Peregrine Bertie, the future Lord Willoughby. Under the influence of the latter's bravery and humor and Bertie's mother, the acute-witted Duchess of Suffolk, the Earl contemplated a reconciliation with the solitary Countess Anne. For the Duchess was an old friend of the Cecils, and maternally sorry for Oxford's wife. In the course of her scheming for their reunion, of which she kept Burghley well informed, he might have tried to assist by letting the Earl learn of Johannes Sturmius's letters inquiring about him and Anne. Two letters written by the German sage on December 4, 1577, leave me with the impression that the writer of *Hamlet* had perused them. They intimated some of Sturmius's anxious thoughts at night about the queens of the English and the Danes. The first went to Sir Francis Walsingham. "In my sleep," said Sturmius, "I wished that the Lord Treasurer was in Denmark with his wife, or someone else of the same rank whose wife could talk Latin; and that such a person should bring from our Queen presents to the King of Denmark's wife...if the minds of kings and men cannot be joined in a league, the minds and affections and loves of queens may be allied. Their solitary lives, their widowhood, when their husbands are dead or dangers arise, are troubles to be dreaded by reason of the changeable wills of men." The sequel letter to Burghley explained that the writer regarded his Lordship's authority and prudence fit to deal masterly with the Danes. But Sturmius wished that Lady Mildred Cecil too could meet the royal pair at Elsinor, because "There is no better hand than that of a wife, especially in the case of husbands who are vehemently in love. As I write this I think of the Earl of Oxford, for I believe his lady speaks Latin also. But these are my wishes; dreams and senile meditations, not counsels."[42] These vagaries of the wise old scholar would have captivated the literary Earl; his mind loved to wander in similar ways, on the wings of meditation and wishes of love.

The excellent plot of the Duchess of Suffolk and her daughter-in-law Mary to restore Lord Edward to marital life dropt to nullity when he met Anne Vavasor, a new attendant in the Queen's bedchamber, and fell amazingly in love. The long and hazardous dance this dark lady led him explains, in my belief, the fire of jealousy—"the pangs of disprized love"—which Hamlet laments to Queen Gertrude in their "closet" or bedchamber talk. The biographic associations with that scene will be treated in due time.

An event which, many scholars are persuaded, appealed to the imagination of Shakespeare a long time before the creation of *Hamlet* occurred on the Avon river on December 17, 1579.

According to an inquest held in February a Warwickshire girl named Katherine Hamlet, "going with a milk-pail to draw water at the river Avon, standing on the bank of the same, suddenly and by accident slipt and fell into the river, and was drowned, and met her death in no other way or fashion."[43] I think that Oxford heard of this during a visit to his rural retreat in Bilton by the Avon. Bilton was a beautiful place, one of the estates that his father had bequeathed for the support of his mother in her widowhood. For various poignant reasons Oxford cherished the manor; it was among the last lands of his heritage that he sold. Bilton seems to be the "seat" that Shakespeare mentions in the Sonnets as his own. Here, within sight of the forest of Arden, the poet, according to my reckoning, first wrote his comedy *As You Like It*.

Early in 1580 the thirty-year-old Oxford occupied himself with reveries and plans to take the leadership of the Court party fighting the Leycester group. The Earl of Sussex was too old and sickly to continue heading that struggle. Urged on by the ingenuity of Lord Henry Howard and Charles Arundel, the dashing Oxford ventured into open conflict with the Dudley faction: he quarreled with Sir Philip Sidney and spurred his players to make fun of his antagonists on the stage. Street fights broke out between his servants and Leycester's partisans from the Inns of Court and blood flowed.

To this year 1580 I ascribe the drama of *Hieronimo*, otherwise famed as *The Spanish Tragedy*, whose author is alleged to be Thomas Kyd. The drama begins with lively reminiscences of the conquest of Portugal by Spain, which took place in August 1580. In a study published in *The Bard* I have given my reasons for crediting the play to Oxford's friend, the scholar Thomas Watson, and dating its first performance at Court on January 1, 1581, when the Earl of Derby's actors entertained Elizabeth. The influence of this tragedy—with its outraged ghost, its father pretending madness while seeking to avenge his murdered son, the faithful friend named Horatio, the play within the play—all this has been sufficiently marked by the experts in Tudor theater. Between *Hieronimo* and *Hamlet* came the composition of Shakespeare's first tragedy, *Titus Andronicus*, done in the shadow of Seneca, but thereby hangs a story told in *Love Lore* of Winter 1968.

While Derby's men were acting their bloody play, De Vere's head was seething with anger against his former comrades, the Howards and Arundels. He had suddenly discovered that they despised him, and were cynic traitors in the service of Roman Catholic statecraft; he went strait to her Majesty with the latter discovery. She demanded evidence, she would not take his word alone. They retaliated with a sequence of lurid charges which have defamed him for nearly four centuries—and incidentally serve to illuminate almost all the works of Shakespeare. By means of such "bugs and goblins" from the life of Hamlet, King Claudius justified his command for the prince's execution in his epistle to England. The counter-charges against Oxford did not all ring false. He found himself so isolated in the Court that he was forced to beg help from his father-in-law. He had only one friend with power left, the Earl of Sussex, and Sussex was getting ready for his grave.

In the spring of 1581 Anne Vavasor gave birth to a male child within the vicinity of the Queen and declared that Oxford was the father. The enraged Elizabeth put them both in the Tower of London. When she released the Earl in July, she ordered him to remain a prisoner at his home in Candlewick Street.[44]

During his banishment George Whetstone's *Heptameron* was printed, a volume of novelets from which came the plot of *Measure for Measure*. In one of Whetstone's moral tales there is an unfortunate wife named Ophella—whom surely Shakespeare had in mind when he named the heroine of *Hamlet*. He probably was aware of the Greek significance of her name; Opheleia means strength and help, "serviceableness," as John Ruskin remarked, pointing to the prophecy of Laertes that his sister would become "a ministering angel" in Paradise.

(Shakespeare would have been somberly amused to learn that the Greek word once meant land-rent, and came from the legendary serpent ophis, said to have served as a watcher (spy) of terrestrial treasures. Hamlet storms at Ophelia for serving as a spy and informer, in cordial innocence of daughterly duty.) In the play she ministers only to the wants of Polonius. Consequently, I guess, Shakespeare meant her name to ring remotely in our ears with the punning sound of "O failure." The proximity of *Hamlet* to *Measure for Measure*, in time as well as temper, is indicated by the tenacity with which the writer's imagination clung to the name Claudio while writing these plays. Claudio happens to be a courtier in Elsinor who receives Hamlet's letters to the King from the sailor who showed them to Horatio. The courtier never comes on the stage. He sends a messenger with the letters to his Majesty, who bears the same name in Latin that he does in Italian.

The tragedy of *Romeo and Juliet* had its counterpart in Edward de Vere's life during March 1582, when he fought a duel with Thomas Knyvet, Anne Vavasor's gallant uncle. Both men were wounded but the Earl got the worst of it.

The summer of 1582 witnessed a bitter argument between Leycester and Sussex over landed property at Havering, Essex, in which Oxford was heartily interested. Elizabeth commanded the contestants to "keep their chambers" and threatened them with prison if they did not yield to her decree for peace. In reporting the affair to Burghley, Walsingham added: "The Queen is resolved not to restore the Earl of Oxford to full liberty till he has been dealt withal for his wife." On which her father remarked in the margin, "This is more easier to be done than courtiers do think."[45]

D

The year 1583 opened with De Vere still in disgrace and his enemies of the Romanist persuasion exerting magnetism on such leaders of the Court as Sir Christopher Hatton and Sir Francis Walsingham. The former had always detested De Vere, who made him hilariously immortal under the mask of Malvolio. Walsingham was never inclined to forgive the strange Earl for making fun of Philip Sidney, his son-in-law. Now the Queen secreted venom against the father of Anne Vavasor's son. His father-in-law lamented, "these advantages are easily gotten where some may say what they will against my Lord of Oxford, and have presence to utter their humors; and my Lord of Oxford is neither heard nor hath presence either to complain or defend himself." Burghley made this lament to Hatton in March. In the same letter he acridly criticized the Earl. Oxford, said he, "hath, I confess, forgotten his duty to God…when our son-in-law was in prosperity, he was cause of our adversity by his unkind usage of us and ours; and now that he is ruined and in adversity, we only are made partakers thereof." Sir Christopher had not the least desire to see the man who had often satirized him restored to the royal smiles. He stimulated the Queen to comment sardonically on De Vere and spread her words as widely as he could. Once she heard about this and reproached him for it. Hatton answered in haste: "if the speech you used of your Turk (one of her nicknames for Oxford) did ever pass my pen or lips to any creature out of your Highness' hearing but to my Lord of Burghley—with whom I have talked both of the man and the matter—I desire no less condemnation than as a traitor."[46]

The nickname Turk merits particular attention in view of Hamlet's odd use of the word after his theatrical success with *The Murder of Gonzago* or *The Mouse Trap.* "Would not this, sir," he asks Horatio, "and a forest of feathers, if the rest of my fortunes turn Turk with me, with two Provincial roses on my razed shoes, get me a fellowship in a cry of players, sir?" An alluring explanation of the nickname finally came from W. Ringland Robinson, an admirer of the Oxford-Shakespeare argument. He discovered in a casual reading of

Walter Scott that the Gaelic word torc, meaning a wild boar, was pronounced Turk. The suggestion led Admiral Hubert Holland to the old Welsh legend of Kilhwch, the hero who earned his bride by capturing a couple of precious articles from the head of the King Boar, Twrch Trwyth (whom Irish folklore called Torc Triath). Holland saw at once that Queen Elizabeth, on learning of this Celtic legend, would have sparkled with pleasure over its links with her madcap Lord of Oxford, whose family emblem was an azure boar and whose motto was *Vero nihil verius, Nothing Truer Than Truth*, or *None Truer Than Vere.*[47] She would have been well aware also that *Torquere* in Latin meant *twist*, and could be punningly applied as a sting with honey to the perversity of her valiant dancer and riming jester, her chief "jig-maker," whom she must have admonished numberless times in the way that Polonius advised Hamlet's mother to warn him:

> Look you, lay home to him,
> Tell him his pranks have been too broad to bear with,
> And that your Grace hath screen'd, and stood between
> Much heat, and him. (Act III, Scene 4)

The poverty of Oxford in this period of lost liberty accounts for the peculiar insistence of Prince Hamlet that he has no money with which to reward his friends. He promises to do for them whatever "so poor a man as Hamlet is" can do. "Beggar that I am," he later asserts, "I am even poor in thanks." Come to think of it, perhaps the tragic speech quoted by Thomas Nash in his allusion to Hamlet, "Blood is a beggar," was actually pronounced by the Prince of Denmark, in one of his money-conscious moods, in a trial text of the play.

In April 1583 another grief made Burghley wish to resign from his offices and retire to the country to die. He lost his second daughter, Lady Elizabeth Wentworth. The Queen gave him permission to leave the Court so he could "wrestle with nature" in privacy,

> When sorrows come, they come not single spies,
> But in battalions.

On April 20 the Earl of Sussex, having made his will, appointed Burghley and Rutland supervisors, prepared for his last journey to Bermondsey, his home in Southwark. His ardent pupil in politics, Oxford, probably accompanied him. Southwark was familiar to both because of the theaters there. Dr. Atslow, the physician of Sussex, was a devout Catholic. His family suffered many state penalties for their faith. Oxford, however, did his best to make them comfortable by grants of land, despite his poverty.

Early in May we find the Earl and his wife residing at his birthplace, Castle Hedingham. The Countess gave birth to a son who lived only two days. They buried the baby Viscount Bulbeck on May 9. Four mournful poems on their loss were published in John Southern's *Pandora* in 1584, a book of verse in broken English by a Frenchman in the service of the Earl. These four lyrics, announced as the Countess's own grieving, show a profound pathos and fine classical education, but they have much more matter than art. In her tears she compares herself to the legendary Niobe, whose image was in Hamlet's thought while he watched his mother at her husband's funeral. The sorrowing Countess also refers to the theory that "our life (may) be caused with moisture and heat"—a line that almost links itself to Hamlet's advice to Polonius not to let his daughter walk in the sun for fear that she might become pregnant from its rays. The destiny that Shakespeare designed for Ophelia was perhaps a poetic retribution for all the eye moisture that his wife had frequently anguished him with.

In May the poet's father-in-law appealed to the rising Walter Ralegh to exploit his personal magic with the Queen for Oxford's sake. Ralegh, remembering Esop's fable of the frozen snake, told Cecil: "I am content for your sake to lay the serpent before the fire, as much as in me lieth, that having recovered strength, myself may be most in danger of his poison and sting." We can estimate the force of Oxford's tongue and pen by the dread they inspired in the witty Master Walter. Nevertheless he liked to see Elizabeth glowing in the radius of his electrical gifts. He pled that she would pardon the Earl and she did. On June 1 her Majesty consoled Lord Burghley at his country mansion Theobalds and "the Earl of Oxford came to her presence, and after some bitter words and speeches, in the end all sins are forgiven, and he may repair to the Court at his pleasure." Roger Manners, who witnessed this scene, declared, "Master Ralegh was a great mean herein, whereat Pondus is angry for that he could not do so much."[48] By Pondus, of course, Manners meant the old man to whom Elizabeth once remarked, "My Lord Burghley, your are burly."

When De Vere returned to the Court he found that Charles Howard, later the Lord Admiral of England, had taken the place of Sussex as Chamberlain of the royal household. The domestic affairs of which the Lord Chamberlain had charge included the production of plays at Court, certainly a task the good sailor Howard was ill qualified for. He would have been grateful to Edward de Vere, the Lord Great Chamberlain of England—whose office involved little labor apart from coronations and parliamentary ceremony—for volunteering to take his theatrical duties off his hands. There was no other man in the Court so profoundly at home in and so fond of the theater.

The Earl of Oxford needed dramatic diversion in June 1583. On the 9th his grand old friend Thomas Radcliff, Earl of Sussex, died of his many painful maladies. The melancholy Oxford saw his last father-figure buried in Boreham, Essex, a few miles from Earls Colne where his own father and ancestors were entombed. I suppose he stood by Sussex's deathbed when the sick warrior is alleged by rumor in the next reign to have uttered his warning against Leycester: "Beware of the Gypsy: you do not know the beast so well as I do." Sinister whispers among the courtiers hinted that Robin Dudley had managed the last agony of Radcliff with the aid of an Italian physician, Julio Borgarucci.[49] The desolate Countess of Sussex became a victim of scandal herself within two months.

During June the Earl of Oxford's troop of actors were strolling in southern England. There was better entertainment available, however, in the debates going on at Oxford University between the doctors of theology and Giordano Bruno, the most fiery of philosophers. They staged a controversy in honor of a foreign guest, Albert Laski, "Count of Polonia." I suspect that it was this Pole, with his stateliness and learning and long beard, who unaware furnished Shakespeare with the stage pattern for his Polonius, a superb caricature of the Lord Treasurer of England. Polonius signifies only a Pole. But who would need to be told that Pole was not a national name in this case, just a joke at the expense of the polished politician Gabriel Harvey once hailed as Polus, the pole-star of England's governmental galaxy, the axle-pin of her cart of state.[50]

On June 20 the lonely De Vere wrote to his father-in-law asking a political kindness for Lord John Lumley, the chief collector of paintings in the kingdom: "For he hath matched with a near kinswoman of mine (Elizabeth Darcy), to whose father I was always beholden unto for his assured and kind disposition unto me." Lord John Darcy, the son of Oxford's aunt Elizabeth, had died the year before. In pleading for Lumley the Earl expressed his sadness because of his other losses in consanguinity.[51] The soldier sons of his uncle Geoffrey, Francis and Horace, whom he had once wished to make his heirs, now were dearer than ever to him.

In June the cleverest of Oxford's enemies, his cousin Lord Henry Howard, issued a pamphlet, "A Defensative against the Poison of Supposed Prophecies." Howard said he wrote it on account of the tragic fate of several of his ancestors, who had fallen into folly and treason as a result of their faith in "old painted books, expositions of dreams, oracles, revelations, invocation of damned spirits…" He alluded with special rancor to the book of prophecies owned by the Earl of Oxford, without mentioning his name. He pretended a surmise that the book was "drawn upon the foresight of one Verdungus, who, during the reign of King Henry VIII, seeking to content and please the moods of certain princes, which were then in dark and deep unkindness with the King, gave out in writing, that the realm should be given up in praedam diversis animantibus (to various creatures for a prey)...the man himself being posted forward with a humor of revenge." After King Henry's death, Howard said, "Verdungus, having made a shameful wreck both of conscience and credit, was scorned and derided for his vain presumption without ground and malice without moderation." The name Verdungus occurs in no chronicle of Tudor history. It appears to be merely a transparent insult to Edward de Vere. The prediction of England's destiny cited by Lord Henry occurs in different forms in the dramas of Shakespeare. Thus it is seen as fulfilled in *Hamlet*:

For thou dost know, O Damon dear,
This real dismantled was
Of Jove himself, and now reigns here
A very, very—pajock.

By "pajock," I conjecture, the poet meant paddock, a kind of toad. One of Hamlet's epithets for his cold-blooded uncle is "paddock." But in the rime he seems to have suppress the word ass.

Howard's "Defensative" was dedicated to Sir Francis Walsingham, since the chief of the Queen's secret service had extended his hand, so the author signed, "to waft me out of the surges of uncertain chance." The phrase appears to hint a distant relation to Shakespeare's "sea of troubles." A closer relation is discernible between Hamlet's sarcasm, "virtue cannot so inoculate our old stock but we shall relish of it," and Howard's flattery of her Majesty, "whose peerless virtues," he proclaimed, "planted in a royal stock, had exempted her from comparison." As I glance again at the title of this treatise, I think that Hamlet's exultant cry, "O my prophetic soul!" represents a defiance of Lord Henry and his fellow critics of the occult.

Early in July her Majesty commanded Oxford's brother-in-law, Lord Willoughby, to sail on an embassy to Denmark. He was to give King Frederick II the royal Order of the Garter and to complain about the Danish treatment of English merchants and mariners, in particular the Danes' severity to the Muscovy Company of London. The King had added insult to injury with a decree that all foreign ships should strike their topsails to Danish men-of-war as a sign of his right to rule the Northern seas. Deeds of tyranny like this burnt in the memories of the men who first heard the King of Denmark in *Hamlet* taunting England with these words:

> thy cicatrice looks raw and red
> After the Danish sword, and thy free awe
> Pays homage to us.

Willoughby landed at Elsinor on July 22. Not until August 14 was the King of the Danes pleased to receive the Garter; then he invited the English ambassador to a royal feast, where soldiers volleyed all the ordnance of the Castle in honor of the King's wassail. The entertainment continued for a few days more—with hunting, drinking endless flagons of Rhenish wine, fireworks and so on—but Willoughby found Frederick practically deaf to his plea for benevolence to the English merchants who desired to trade with Russia. Finally he said farewell, and by the end of September arrived home in London to report on his embassy, and regale his kin and comrades with merry description of the Danes.

During the spring of 1583 the Earl of Leycester strove to arrange a wedding between Dorothy Devereux, his stepdaughter, and James Stewart, King of Scots. In July the gallant Thomas Perrot, who held an obscure office in Robert Dudley's service, exploded his lofty plans by eloping with his stepdaughter. Admiral Hubert H. Holland, in his pioneer volume *Shakespeare Through Oxford Glasses* (London 1924) discerned a series of subtle witty references to this affair in the seemingly crazy outcries of Ophelia to Claudius and Gertrude:

> You must sing down-a-down,
> And you call him a-down-a.
> Mark how the wheel becomes it! This is the false steward that stole his master's daughter…O! you must wear your rue with a difference.
>
> (Act IV, Scene 5)

Concurrent with the meaning of her lines for the King and Queen, which I will deal with later, we have, as Admiral Holland pointed out first, allusions to the diverting of Dorothy Devereux from her stepfather's marital plot. The Perrots were accustomed to hearing their name pronounced Parrot, which in Italian, Holland observed, would become Parrota and signify an equal or peer wheel, thus justifying Ophelia's avowal that "the wheel becomes it"—the worthy Parrot deserved his Dorothy. And "rue with a difference," Holland noted, turned in French to divers rue—a pun on the runaway bride's name.

When Holland made this observation he had no knowledge of the place Parrot held in Leycester's household. He guessed that Parrot was a servant, despite the Elizabethan annals where he is alleged to have been an obscure worker for the Queen's wages. In support of this surmise I offer the fact that Perrot walked among the mourners at the funeral of Sir Philip Sidney in the same rank with Edward Waterhouse, the steward of Sidney's father. In the illumination of these facts the moral-satiric purpose, the dramatic method in the madness of Ophelia emerges clear as day.

In September 1583 the Count of Polonia, Albert Laski, left England with Dr John Dee and Edward Kelly, Dee's disciple in alchemy. Our dramatist could now consider in earnest the stage possibilities of the Pole's face and stature for masking his portrait of Burghley's soul. In the same month Oxford sold to Roger Harlackenden, a former steward, the manor and park of Earls Colne, which embraced the burial building of the Earls of Oxford. While executing this break with tradition, he served on a commission in Colchester to enroll recruits in the army. Rumors of war increased in the country, tho people disagreed about the state on which the English steel would fall. The folk anxiety made the war that Denmark was waging in Livonia, Poland seem very far away. It impressed only a small number of international minds on the island. It supplied Shakespeare with a motive for Prince Fortinbras's march across Denmark.

De Vere's imagination at this time was provoked by more than military affairs or the selling of his family lands. He must have meditated passionately on the virtual imprisonment of Lady Frances, the widow of Sussex in her house near the theaters of Southwark. The Queen had ordered the widow to remain there indoors because of a Court accusation that she had been faithless to her husband. A letter which Lady Frances sent to Elizabeth, of which Kit Hatton kept a copy, reveals her trouble and appeals for pity. She wrote in despair against the "sinister suggestion, I should be defamed to be undutiful to your most excellent Majesty, and injurious to the honor of my dear Lord lately deceased." The Countess named not one of her defamers, but we may guess that they belonged to the Howard fraternity. After all, she was born and bred a Sidney, and therefore could be tarred with the same brush they lustily employed against Sir Philip's uncle and Leycester's wives. We learn from the widow's appeal that the calumniators had reached her husband's ear before he died. They "long complotted my ruin," she mourned; they "espied their time when my Lord, through anguish and torments was brought to his utmost weakness, to break the perfect bond and love of twenty-eight years continuance...which bringeth on every side such a sea of sorrows as, were it not for the fear of God's revenge, I could with all heart redeem them with the sacrifice of my life."[52] Is it not likely that we have here the source of the "sea of troubles" in Hamlet's soliloquy, or his earlier lament that the Everlasting had fixt "His canon 'gainst self-slaughter"? Edward de Vere may have been privileged to listen to the widow's distress before she begged Hatton and Elizabeth for redemption. And meditating on her woes he would have remembered how he had tortured his own wife with charges of infidelity.—"If thou dost marry...be thou as chaste as ice, as pure as snow, thou shalt not escape calumny."

Presumably Oxford turned to literature to assist him in forgetting the griefs of the living which afflicted him. Surely he read Robert Greene's romance *Mamillia*, whose second part came from the press in the autumn of 1583, with its sad tale of the slandered Publia. Elements of Greene's novel seem to have gone into the making of *Hamlet*. Gostino, for example, like Polonius, "sifts" his daughter, Publia, to learn the extent of her love for young Pharicles. Gostino's brother Gonzaga—a name that conjures for us the royal family of Hamlet's "Mouse Trap"—had informed him that evil rumors were spoken about the girl. Obediently she gives up to her father her lover's letters. And after Gostino's death she enters a nunnery, the refuge that Hamlet urged in vain for Ophelia.

In my belief, the Earl of Oxford, reflecting on his brother-in-law's adventures in Denmark and the book of Belleforest containing the history of Hamlet engendered the early version of his tragedy of the Dane. I think he conceived it while resorting, for an antidote to depression, to a beloved playhouse.

In the winter of 1583 the children who served him as actors rehearsed two plays for the Court. The royal treasury paid his secretary John Lyly twenty pounds for their performances. One took place on New Year's night and the other on March 3. The anonymous romance called *The Weakest Goeth to the Wall* (which the eminent Shakespearean authority E. K. Chambers conjectured might be the work of Oxford himself, but which I believe came from the pen of Anthony Mundy) could have been played by the Earl's boys on one of these nights. It deals with a noble couple divided by treason, poverty and other disasters, who come together again and win felicity at last.

The Earl had another company of actors touring the provinces in this season, a company of men. Very little is known about them except that they favored for theatric use the innyard of the Boar's Head Tavern. I like to suppose that they are "the tragedians of the city" whose talents Hamlet took such delight in. He calls their First Player "old friend," and discloses an intimate knowledge of their roles and abilities. We are told that they have been compelled to leave the city and travel;—in the words of the first quarto of the play—"The principal public audience that came to them are turned to private plays and to the humor of children." They called plays private when performed in exclusive, top-priced chambers like the Blackfriars, not in the common playhouses and innyards.

When Hamlet's tragedians visit him in Elsinor, their country is industriously preparing for a war with an unnamed land, Norway, according to some. England, in the beginning of 1584, busied herself with preparations for battle after the Spanish ambassador Mendoza was expelled for complicity in plots against Elizabeth's life. In February financiers of Antwerp heard "that the country is entirely shut off." In May their letters from London announced that the city was mobilizing three thousand men, "presumably against Scotland."[53] These armaments and rumors must have reminded Edward de Vere of his single military experience, when he rode north in April 1570 to follow the idolized Earl of Sussex in his border campaign.

February 1584 saw the sale of more of Oxford's land. With what vitriolic humor he observed the parchment scribbling, scrutinies and debates of the lawyers and landlords with whom he dealt, we can tell with ease, having the deliberate laughter of Hamlet at real estate before us. The poet could not share the raptures of William Shakspere of Warwickshire over being "spacious in the possession of dirt." And he wanted money to invest in the "Fellowship for the Discovery of the North-west Passage," which attempted to reach the Orient by way of Arctic waters in the following year. This was not the first time the Earl poured hundreds of pounds from many a goodly manor he sold into a voyage for the Northwest Passage dream. He could not resist the fascination of sea captains and explorers who talked quite practically of penetrating those "unpath'd waters and undream'd of shores." Hamlet's common-sense was unstrung in the same way: "I am but mad north-north-west: when the wind is southerly, I know a hawk from a handsaw." (The latter is a sort of heron.) Among Oxford's colleagues in the Fellowship for finding a way to India thru ice were the Earl of Leicester, his nephew Philip Sidney, Walter Ralegh, Francis Drake, the recluse Edward Dyer, and their mystic friend Dr John Dee. What would we not give for a transcript of one conversation about the voyage held by these infinitely interesting men!

On February 18, 1584 Henry Vavasor, the father of Earl Edward's sweetheart Anne, died in his home at Copmansthorp, York. Her brother Thomas, a young firebrand who experienced some hardship from the government because of his Roman Catholic loyalties, inherited the Vavasor estate. The life of a country gentleman did not suit his temperament; so he came to London and entered the service of the Earl of Warwick,

Leycester's brother. He also undertook to wield his blade against anybody who used his "natural sister"Anne for ungodly purposes, in particular the father of her bastard son Edward Vere. I believe that she tried to sever all love-ties with the Earl of Oxford after her father's death. Within a month, I guess, she became the paramour of John Finch, a merchant trading with Muscovy, or maybe she chose to become the mistress of Sir Henry Lee, the Queen's Champion in tournaments, who had to ride against Thomas Vavasor in one of these chivalric sports in December of 1584. February and March must have been months of bitter sexual deprivation for Oxford. The Countess Anne was then pregnant with his second daughter, Bridget.

During the period Burghley's second son Robert was pursuing his studies in Paris, but we do not know what agent of his father spied on him. Robert Cecil hardly resembled his half-brother Thomas. His presence in Paris however would have recalled to De Vere the days of father William's fretting about Thomas while lodging at Castle Hedingham. Old "Pondus" this season had worse things to worry about. For his son-in-law seems to have struggled to renew his mind's union with the mother of his only son. Thomas Vavasor raged against the Earl for "spotting" his house and demanded to cross swords with him, in vain.

At this point I will offer a fancy of mine to explain why Shakespeare chose the name Laertes for the brother of Hamlet's nymph. It struck me that "Laertes" is an anagram for "all are Ts." (The anagram is a little plainer when the name is pronounced in Elizabethan fashion, Leartes, as spelled in the quarto of 1602.) I imagine it occurred to the Earl of Oxford as odd that the three young men who detested him most fiercely for his treatment of Anne Cecil de Vere and her rival Anne were each named Thomas: Cecil, Knyvet and Vavasor. If he thought of their initials he may have been amused by the similarity in sound between "all are Ts" and the Greek name he picked for his Danish duelist.

E

The date I propose for the starting point of the composition of *Hamlet* is Tuesday, March 17, 1584. Saint Patrick's day. There seems to me no other plausible reason for the hero's swearing by Saint Patrick after the conversation with his father's ghost. Several references to the month or weather of March appear casually in the play. In the opening scene the memory of Julius Caesar's murder is evoked, the unforgettable deed of the Ides of March (March 15). Later we learn that Polonius acted the death of Caesar at his university. A Latin tragedy about the assassination was played at Oxford University in 1582. If my reckoning is right, on the anniversary of that event the ghost of King Hamlet first walked the parapets of Elsinor Castle, on the platform of our dramatist's fantasy. Two nights before the dawn of the drama the armed fantom was seen by the sentinels. The downfall of the supreme Roman associated in Shakespeare's mind with the agonized death of the Dane.

He also gave some thought to the compulsory fasting in Christendom this month. Rosencrantz pretends to wonder "what Lenten entertainment the players shall receive" from the Prince. Possibly the tedium of his diet in Lent provoked Hamlet's insult to Polonius: "You are a fishmonger." We can see Cecil frowning on his son-in-law's preference for caviar, of which we get a hint in Thomas Nash's allusion to the appetite of De Vere as he witnessed it in the tavern of the Steelyard, the Baltic marketplace in London.[54] The frequent references to food in our drama may all be products of the poet's March fast.

Prior to April 11, when Robert Greene's romance *Gwidonius; The Card of Fancy* was licensed for the press, Oxford accepted the dedication of the book. It is noteworthy that theatrical imagery first turns up in Greene's works in *Gwidonius*, when he gained Oxford as a patron of his pen. Our poet perhaps had Greene's title in view when he made Osric say about Laertes, "he is the card or calendar of gentry." From the same novel Shakespeare may have drawn the name of Lucianus for his drama, and his idea of a scene where a father delivers precepts to a son going abroad.

If the dramatist's portrayal of King Hamlet's jester, Sir Yorick, was intended (as many scholars surmise) for a tribute to Will Summers, the court clown of King Henry VIII, this would be additional evidence for my chronology of the play. The bones of poor Yorick, we are told, have lain in the churchyard 22 years. Will Summers was buried on June 15, 1560, in the churchyard of St Leonard in Shoreditch, the very ground where Queen Elizabeth's clown Dick Tarlton was buried in 1588. A number of eminent actors made their homes in the parish of St. Leonard, including veterans of the Chamberlain's company. Some day researchers in the documents of Will Summers may exhume a testimony that, after the death of Henry VIII, the jester joined the players belonging to the earldom of De Vere, and perhaps used to set the banqueters at Castle Hedingham roaring with mirth when Earl Edward was a child. Meanwhile let us contemplate for a moment the fact that the human race's supreme artist paused in writing his most memorable work to recall the funeral of a cherished fool twenty-three years before. In Shakespeare's time and territory, remember, the year was not yet 1584. He would use the calendar of the courts and number it 1583 until March 25, the vernal equinox.

By the exact calculation of the second quarto of *Hamlet*, the hero is only thirty years old. On the day King Hamlet defeated King Fortinbras of Norway in a single combat, the First Clown became a sexton in the tragedy and Prince Hamlet was born. These events took place thirty years before the funeral of Ophelia. Oxford had not reached his 34th birthday when he created the Prince of Denmark. The poet's emphasis on "thirty" points to something more vital than a round figure for his hero's age. It appears to me that Shakespeare revealed by this reckoning his obsessional remembrance of the crisis that altered his life so radically by 1580. "By the Lord, Horatio," cries the Prince, "these three years I have taken note of it: the age is grown so picked that the toe of the peasant comes so near the heel of the courtier, he galls his kibe." If we had the "pleasant conceit of Vere, Earl of Oxford, discontented at the rising of a mean gentleman in the English Court, circa 1580," which Francis Peck promised to print (in 1732) and did not, we would today have a good glimpse of the notes which the poet had taken down in his tables on the presumption of the "peasantry" and vulgar gentry toward the courtiers. He must have kept foremost in his thought the rebuke Queen Elizabeth delivered to Philip Sidney after the latter's tennis-court dispute with Oxford in the summer of 1579: "There is a great difference in degree," she insisted, "between the Earls and private gentlemen, and Princes are bound to support the nobility and to insist on their being treated with proper respect."[55] The frequently quoted but seldom thought about speech in *Troilus and Cressida* on social rank and grade endeavors to elucidate the cruciality of the classes.

When *Hamlet* was originally conceived, the author was not so much concerned about lessons and laughing-stock of class distinction as he was with feuds and revenge on his "mighty opposites" in the state. He burnt for vengeance on Lord Henry Howard and his partisans. The exposure of the Throgmorton conspiracy in November 1583 gave him the chance he craved. Charles Arundel was deeply implicated in this plot to enthrone Mary Stuart and restore the Pope's sovrenty to the English church, and he fled to France to escape the royal ax. Lord Howard managed to keep his connection with Throgmorton well concealed. But under suspicion of treason he was held a prisoner for about seven months while he endured an inquisition spearheaded by questions that Oxford supplied. He occupied a room in the Tower of London in February 1584. Maybe there were more drastic achievements to satisfy the Earl's yearning for the ruin of his Romanist enemies: For one of them, Thomas Vavasor, wrote to him in January 1585 demanding: "Is not the revenge taken of thy victims sufficient?"[56]

The Earl craved vengeance on the Earl of Leycester too, since the death of Sussex, the breaking of the Howard faction, and Oxford's own disgrace had left Lord Robert the cheeriest cock of the Court walk. Sussex had died knowing that Lord Edward could never succeed him in the leadership of the fight against Leycester. Realizing that he had failed, Edward became depressed: "I have of late—but wherefore I know not—lost all my mirth, forgone all custom of exercises." Naturally he hunted for creatures on whom he could discharge his pent wrath; finding none to whom he would be pitiless, like the savage Greek Pyrrhus, whose feats at Troy Hamlet could not forget, he turned for relief to slaughter in effigy: he spilled ink-blood in a tragedy.

An idea obtrudes itself that he was inspired on the midnight of Sunday, March 15, by an apparition of Thomas Radcliff, which seemed to appeal for revenge on her Majesty's darling Dudley, since he (so it was whispered) had put an end to the suffering of Sussex by a dram Doctor Julio distilled. In the Earl's mind's ears also reverberated the sorrowing of Radcliff's Countess and the murmurs of her alleged affair with someone of Leycester's circle—Roger, Lord North maybe, whom her husband had often denounced a "knave," or maybe the magnificent Robin himself. I do not think that De Vere believed in ghosts. But he believed in himself and the magic power of his tongue and quill to destroy any person who barred his path. He apparently imagined that Dudley was the main fellow standing in the path to fulfillment of his ambition to become a general beloved by the Queen.

While *Hamlet* was in the making a letter arrived from Sturmius to Elizabeth, pleading for her military assistance to the Netherlands. The Protestant leader urged her to send a cavalry expedition against the Spaniards, and recommended for command of her horsemen "some faithful and zealous personage, such as the Earl of Oxford, the Earl of Leycester, or Philip Sidney." It might have been this letter that spurred Oxford to return to his equestrian exercises. In November 1584 he rode for the third time in his life in a tournament before the Queen, and for the third time won the main prize by his skill in breaking lances and managing steeds. Conceive then of his sentiments on seeing the Earl of Leycester by the side of her Majesty directing the tournament as the Master of the Horse.[57] Charles Arundel charged that Oxford "forgeth out of his own giddy brain what he taketh to be fittest for the speeding of his ancient friends"—and foes too, of course. "By devising tales and lies," wrote Arundel, "he would set one man to kill another." Ideas of assassinating Leycester pleased him particularly. Once he proposed to Lord Henry Howard a scheme "to make Leyster be killed at the Garden Staire (opposite Sussex House on the Thames) as he landed from my Lord of Essex." Howard also reported a device that Oxford allegedly worked out "with certain cutters to set up Leyster" on his road to Wanstead "and to murder him." The reason for these daydreams, according to Arundel, was brutal jealousy. De Vere was infuriated because Dudley "boasted"—so De Vere told Arundel—"of his greatness in alliance, wealth, credit with the Queen, etc." Leycester affirmed that he was able to make the proudest subject to sweat that would oppose himself against him. De Vere's hatred of Dudley started, I reckon, in his thirteenth year, when every acre, "all and singular (lands) there appertaining in the counties of Essex, Suffolk, and Cambridgeshire, late the inheritance of the Right Hon. John de Vere Earl of Oxford," were put under the control of Robert Dudley, Elizabeth's lover.[58]

The poet accused his rival, in the person of King Claudius, of his own guilty aspiration, the aspiration branded by Belleforest in his foreword to the history of *Hamlet* "the abominable vice of desire to reign." Shakespeare chose this history for his plot in order to show England the divine vengeance bound to fall on the men who (in Belleforest's words) "spill the blood of their nearest kinsmen and friends, to attain to the honor of being great and in authority." *Der Bestrafte Brudermord*, that primitive German version of *Hamlet*, concludes with this piece of morality, recited by Horatio:

> So goes it when a king by craft attempts to get the throne,
> And treacherously triumphs in making it his own;
> He nothing gains himself but jeers and mocking rage,
> For worthy of the labor, always follows due the wage.

The manuscript of the German *Hamlet* is dated 1710 but all scholars are convinced that it represents the earthly remains of the *Tragedy of Hamlet, Prince of Denmark* which was acted in Dresden in 1626 by a troop of wandering Englishmen. "Fratricide Punished" exhibits a fidelity to Belleforest and a semblance of the first quarto of *Hamlet* which point to its priority of conception in the development of the play. From its pages may be deduced what the earliest London Audience of *Hamlet* witnessed at the Theater in the fall of 1584.

The "Fratricide" opens with a vision of the Near Orient goddess of night, the very divinity whose radiance prevails over the *Comedy of Errors*, the romance of *Pericles*, and other productions by Shakespeare. This time she comes forth in the shape of black Hecate, the deity of *Macbeth*, mounted on a chariot decorated with stars. She conjures the three sisters, the Furies, to view with her the castle of Elsinor, murmuring peacefully under its shadows of murder and lust, and she summons them to revenge.

When these she-fiends are gone, we see two sentinels of the castle, Francisco and Horatio, on guard. Horatio here is a soldier, just returned from inspecting the night watch. Later we hear Prince Hamlet praise him for doing the duty of "an honorable soldier, on whose arms the safety of the King and realm depends." Francisco and Horatio unquestionably stand for those two brave guardians of England, Francis and Horace Vere. First cousins of the Earl of Oxford, these brothers always acted as upholders of his house, tho they earned wages most of their lives as soldiers under foreign flags. Francis in the spring of 1584 was 24 years old and a captain with the English volunteers in the Netherlands. Horace—or Horatio, as he is sometimes called in government records—was only nineteen, but he already manifested the calm temperament and serene head that made him superior to his brother in war. Shakespeare has portrayed them both with a few rare strokes of his art. Thus Francisco's speech, "'Tis bitter cold, and I am sick at heart," sounds exactly like the complaints the English and Dutch were accustomed to hear from the moody Francis Vere. On the other hand, as Looney was the first to point out, Hamlet's description of his confidant Horatio fits no contemporary so well as brother Horace:

> Since my dear soul was mistress of her choice
> And could of men distinguish, her election
> Hath seal'd thee for herself, for thou hast been
> As one, in suffering all, that suffers nothing,
> A man that fortune's buffets and rewards
> Hast ta'en with equal thanks.

This is how the historian Thomas Fuller, in the generation after Horace Vere's, described him: "Sir Horace had more meekness and as much valor as his brother; so pious that he first made his peace with God before he went out to war with man. One of an excellent temper, it being true of him what is said of the Caspian Sea, 'that it doth never ebb nor flow'; observing a constant tenor, neither elated nor depressed with success."[59] Shakespeare thought of his Horatio as a sort of feudal comrade and servant, devoted to Hamlet so perfectly that (like King

Lear's dogged retinue leader Kent) he could barely exist without the Prince. Watching his master die, Horatio declares, "I am more an antique Roman than a Dane." He wants to follow Hamlet in death like the servant of the regicide Brutus followed his leader at Philippi. The poets who knew Sir Horace Vere were all conscious of his Roman-like dignity. Ben Jonson wrote an epigram extolling him for it:

> Which of thy names I take, not only bears
> A Roman sound, but Roman virtue wears,
> Illustrious Vere, or Horace.

We know how much Shakespeare valued this Roman virtue. Edward de Vere also must have claimed, "I am more an antique Roman than a Dane." Percy Allen has shown that a paternal tradition in the Earl's family laid claim to an origin in pagan Rome, while from his mother's side, as the name Golding hints, Edward had Danish blood.[60]

The warrior Veres were in London in the winter of 1584. They acted as messengers of the Earl to Thomas Vavasor. Striving to cool his ire, they—or rather Francis—stoked it up. Vavasor challenged Oxford to tell why he used these "unworthy instruments to provoke my unwilling mind? Or dost thou fear thyself, and therefore has sent thy forlorn kindred, whom as thou hast left nothing to inherit, so thou dost thrust them violently into thy shameful quarrels?"[61]

Let me digress again at this moment to indicate likely historic sources of the other two guards at Shakespeare's Elsinore. Marcellus, I assume, was named after Marcellus Bax, the Dutch hero who often marched to battle by the side of the brothers Vere. And the poet, in my opinion, formed the name of Bernardo from that of another champion of the Dutch revolution, John of Barnevelt. Oddly enough, in a translation of *Hamlet* printed in Hamburg 1778, the soldier's name is given as Bernefeld.

The two sentinels of *Der Bestrafte Brudermord* walk in darkness and cold, listening to the noise of royal merriment below, and they talk of the warlike Ghost of their late King, which they alone have seen. Suddenly Prince Hamlet comes on the platform, greets the soldiers, and enters with them in a discussion of politics. We learn that Hamlet's father had died while he was studying in Germany. His uncle Erico then "had himself quickly crowned king in Denmark, but with a show of justice," Hamlet adds, "he has made over to me the crown of Norway and appealed to the election of the states." The Ghost emerges and at once our hero shows himself a man of action: "The Ghost beckons me, Gentlemen, stand apart a while: Horatio, do not go too far. I will follow the Ghost and see what he wants." With cool valor the lone prince attends to the fantom's detailed report of his death by poisoning at the hands of brother Erico. The murder weapon is called the juice of Ebeno, that is ebony, about whose potency Shakespeare had learnt in the book of Bartholomaeus "On the Properties of Things," translated by Stephen Batman and issued in 1582. In selecting this venom for the crime the dramatist may have dimly remembered the passage in the old poem *Confessio Amantis*, by Chaucer's friend John Gower, where the couch of the god of sleep is said to be made of "Hebenus, that sleepy tree."[62]

The Ghost calls King Erico "my crown-coveting brother," but says nothing about incest and hardly a dozen words about the seduction of Sigrie, his queen. He concludes the account of his murder with a sentence that Shakespeare did not improve in the subsequent revisions of his play: "Thus was I by this tyrant of crown, of queen, of life at once deprived."

Savagely the fantom demands revenge; the prince vows to spend his whole life in pursuit of the new king's blood. In the original English the Ghost must have given Hamlet a signal and a slogan for the cause to which his days will be dedicated: Vindicta! Contemporary allusions to the tragedy usually recall this Latin cry for vengeance. Thus Ben Jonson's comedy *Poetaster*, acted by the Queen's Chapel children in 1601, has a character shout: "The Ghost, boys !—Vindicta!" The anonymous drama *A Warning for Fair Women*, also acted by competitors of the Lord Chamberlain's men, begins with ridicule of our play, sneering at tragedies that show

> How some damn'd tyrant to obtain a crown
> Stabs, hangs, impoisons, smothers, cutteth throats.
> Then too, a filthy whining ghost,
> Lapt in some foul sheet, or a leather pilch,
> Comes screaming like a pig half-stick'd,
> And cries, Vindicta!—Revenge, revenge!

When Hamlet returns to his armored friends in the German version, Francisco promises to help him in any enterprise of feud he will attempt: "Your highness knows the great love I bear you. I will risk my life willingly if you wish to avenge yourself." He and Horatio swear to be loyal on the prince's sword, but Hamlet does not reveal the fantom's story to Francisco. He confides in none but Horatio. "My father— "Hamlet tells him, "he who is now my father" murdered the late king. Several times in the *Brudermord*, and in the first quarto, Hamlet calls the assassin "father," a filial-self-betraying habit that Shakespeare extinguished in his final reform of the tragedy. In the German drama the prince proceeds to review the difficulties of his task. He announces to Horatio that he will simulate madness in order to fool the king into believing him harmless. "My father," says he, "is always surrounded by many guards." He will have to be wary in hunting for the chance to strike the fratricide down. Perhaps he will fail and be killed: "Should you chance to find my dead body, let it be buried honorably." There is no doubt that in *Fratricide Punished* the sole reason for Hamlet's delay in killing his uncle is the circumstance that the villain goes always protected by his Switzers, the bodyguard conspicuous by their absence in the quarto of 1604.

The German *Hamlet* picks Ophelia as the first target of his mock-madness. He chases her thru the Court, apparently with a hope of sexual surprise. At the command of her father, Corambus, she returns a jewel the prince had given her, and he pours on the girl's head a tirade against her sex. "Go to a nunnery!" he thunders. The eavesdropping king informs Corambus that he thinks Hamlet's madness mere dissembling; he resolves to get rid of his nephew.

In the course of this Hamlet's polemic against women, he tells Ophelia the anecdote of the cavalier of Anion (Anjou?) who married a lady famous for corporeal beauty. On going to bed the knight observed to his horror that his wife extracted a glass eye and false teeth and washed away as paint the fine color of her face. A specter presented herself to the groom—a bride of shreds and patches! The prince's sarcasm on cosmetics, which Shakespeare maintained in the later versions of *Hamlet*, made a sharp impression on Robert Greene, an author noted for his defense of feminine liberties. In his *Planetomachia*, printed in 1585, Greene deplores face-painting as "a disease rooted in women from their swathing clouts, and not worn out until they come in their winding sheet." This is the earliest reference to cosmetics in Greene's books, which aimed primarily to please the ladies.

The *Planetomachia* contains another passage that reminds us of Hamlet. Speaking of men over whose destiny the star of Venus rules, Greene depicts them "carrying honey in their mouths, and like spaniels flattering with their tails." Here we have that strange association of the sweet tongue and doglike servility to superiors which the pioneer psychologian Walter Whiter, and long afterward Caroline Spurgeon, proved peculiar to Shakespeare's thought.[62a]

We go back to the *Brudermord*: Before King Erico can act on his resolution to do away with Hamlet, the prince springs his dumbshow trap. It is preceded by talk of Roscius, Jephthah, and Pyrrhus, which clearly points to Shakespeare's own *Hamlet* as the source of *Fratricide Punished.* The dumbshow by itself scares the king into flight, crying for torches. Then Charles, the prudent leader of the actors, asks Hamlet for a passport. The prince praises their quality to Chamberlain Corambus, and their unique contribution to culture. Without an invitation, he goes to his mother's room. Here he exhibits an extraordinary caution. "Hush!" he admonishes the queen. "Are the doors shut fast?" The courtier-spy behind the curtain coughs and the prince stabs him.

In Saxo Grammaticus's chronicle of Denmark the counselor-spy concealed himself under straw in mother Geruth's room. Amleth dances on the straw and so discovers him. Belleforest made the hiding place the queen's quilt. Shakespeare would never permit the royal bed of Denmark to be a couch for espionage. He invented the concealment behind the tapestry. Yet the first quarto still kept Hamlet's precaution. When the queen requires an explanation for his wild conduct, he answers, "I'll tell you, but first we'll make all safe"—presumably bolting the doors. Up to the quarto of 1604 the prince sustains the character of a careful, remorseless man, by no means the overflowing soul, "free from all contriving," whom Shakespeare fashioned for us in his last *Hamlet.*

The son of Queen Sigrie, pointing to the "counterfeit" of her first husband hanging in her gallery, attacks her for having held the funeral of that king and her nuptials with his successor on the very same day! The Ghost appears in the chamber—in a glare of lightning—but says not one word. The hero is nevertheless reminded that his mother must be left to heavenly justice while he should restrict his energy to regicide. The queen cannot see her dead husband's spirit. "You are no longer worthy to look on his figure," her son asserts. "Not one more word will I speak unto you." He leaves Sigrie consoling herself with the memory of the Pope's sanction of her second marriage.

The crude sketch of the *Brudermord* next carries Hamlet off to sea, accompanied by two scoundrels whom the monarch has ordered to kill the prince. Not far from Dover they are forced ashore by contrary winds. They find themselves on a desolate island (off the coast of Essex?). The brigands, at opposite ends of the state, announce their intention of shooting Hamlet, but he persuades them to hold their harquebus fire until he gives the signal to shoot. At the instant he does so, the hero throws himself on the ground and the bullets dispose of both ruffians at once. "Now," Hamlet calmly remarks, "I will return to my father—to his horror." By this trick the playwright deprived his protagonist of the adventures in England narrated in Belleforest, including the marriage which happily omened the victory of Hamlet in Elsinore. The poet's intervention with the pirates in the two quartos hardly marks an advance in his stagecraft. However, as W. S. Gilbert remarked on a certain tragedian's performance of *Hamlet*, it is funny without being vulgar, which cannot be said of the shooting episode.

On landing again in Denmark the prince of the German tragedy calls out to the goddess of revenge: "How long, O Nemesis, wilt thou delay before thou whet'st thy sword of righteous vengeance against my uncle, the brother-slayer?" Once more he excuses the delay by reference, not to the divinity, but the crowd of armed hirelings who hedge the king.

Meanwhile Corambus's son Leonhardus has come back from France, heard the story of his father's disgraceful death, and seen his sister Ophelia in the throes of insanity. The "Fratricide" nowhere suggests that the death of Corambus played any part in blasting her wits. She raves about a lover not named. And her author makes her an object of Bedlam humor, having her chase after the comic courtier Phantasmo (afterward named Osric) with amorous beck and shriek. Thus the poet punished Ophelia for her attempt to seduce Hamlet and her compliance with the plotting of her father and the king. The girl's agony ends with the dashing out of her brains by suicide from a high hill. Leonhardus, thirsty for retribution, quickly turns into a tool of the tyrant, who proposes to him the device of the venomed sword as well as the poisoned cup. When Hamlet hears of Leonhardus's invitation to the swords, he faints and blood runs from his nose—an omen of his own end. They exchange blades in the contest and both are fatally hurt. After the queen drinks from the deadly cup Hamlet at last stabs her husband—from behind: "thou, tyrant, shalt bear her company in death." Incidentally he kills Osric, or rather Phantasmo, too, because that gentleman brought the poisoned sword. The prince bequeaths the Danish crown to his cousin Fortempras of Norway, and dies. Then Horatio laments the atrocities that have happened to the kingdom, so soon after the close of a hard war.

A remarkable difference between Shakespeare's plot and his raw material is the change he worked in the role of the queen. In the Danish original she is socially the superior of her two husbands. They are only dukes of provinces under her father, the overlord of Denmark They attain the crown, it seems, by right of marriage with Geruth, for the people still uphold the tribal principle of matrilineal inheritance. This is precisely the same principle that gave young Oedipus, the son and mate of Iocasta, the throne of Thebes. Shakespeare left the lineage of his Gertrude in the dark.

Our dramatist did more than change the happy ending in Belleforest's history into a somber and bloody event. He converted the death of Hamlet's father from butchery done in the open at a feast to a crafty assassination in solitude. By this metamorphosis he technically justified the appearance of his Ghost, the sole means of communicating to Hamlet the method of the regicide. By making the murder a secret, however, Shakespeare multiplied the perils of his hero. For Hamlet's assumed madness or "antic disposition" then became a handicap instead of a trick to look harmless and save him from distrust. It invited suspicion. His uncle now had good cause to be watchful toward the formerly bright boy. But our poet could not bear to part with this posture of folly which Belleforest had furnished him. It reminded him of the imbecile mask worn by the patriot Junius Brutus when he conspired to drive the tyrant Tarquin out of Rome—a feat celebrated in *The Rape of Lucrece*. Moreover it gave the dramatist the pretext he sorely wanted to carry out the program of satire and social therapy which he had meditated in *As You Like It*:

> In vest in me my motley, give me leave
> To speak my mind, and I will through and through
> Cleanse the foul body of the infected world,
> If they will patiently receive my medicine.

This mask of motley was the Earl of Oxford's own disguise of aggression, in fact his ego integument. It endowed him with the check that Gabriel Harvey, in *The Mirror of Tuscanismo* (1580), called his "smirking physiognomy." The vision of this countenance was surely in the mind's eye of Lord Burghley when he instructed his son Robert: "Be not scurrilous in thy conversation, nor satirical in thy jests…I have seen many so prone to quip and gird as they would rather lose their friend than their jest. And if by chance their boiling brains yield any quant scoff, they will travail to be delivered of it, as a woman with child."[63] To my view, the humor of Hamlet, more than his passion or intellect or anything else, is the factor that turns his tragedy into the author's autobiography.

II.

To the Subliminal

Laughter means abrupt relief from anxiety: it explodes a respiration which has been constricted by fear. The sudden revelation that we are not really in danger frees the breath along with an outburst of defiance, combining sob and taunt. A humorist generally searches for and provokes situations that approximate danger for the sake of enjoying his elusion and a fresh feeling of security. If his quests and provocations disappoint him, he is driven to invent these predicaments on the stage of his soul. Eventually he might render them in literature.

Well, what peril was Edward de Vere in when he felt the necessity of producing *Hamlet*? We know of nothing in his external conditions in March 1584 which could have pricked him into writing it. After his banishment from the Court he probably trod warily, denying himself the thrills of many a temptation to hunt or kindle his favorite types of trouble. He had to be provident for his skin, which still carried the cicatrice of Thomas Knyvet's steel. His encounter with Master Tom's rapier and dagger had brought him to the edge of death. It caused him to reflect how fatal a mere scratch might be. "I do not set my life at a pin's fee," Hamlet says; yet his thought continually returns to the power of a pin in the flesh of a prince. He broods on the efficacy of "a bare bodkin" for concluding one's ordeals in this world. He even swears by "God's bodkin," punning on the idea of his God's little body and this concept of the pin. In the end he receives his deadly wound from the point of Laertes' sword. The way our dramatist dwells on the potency of a skin-tear leads me to believe that he must have been obsessed with the memory of his duel and the question, why did he fail to kill? He had plenty of reasons for hating Knyvet and killed him in fantasy countless times (for instance, in *Romeo and Juliet*). I conjecture that during the fight he had experienced a queer inhibition, a backward pull of his blade, when he might have executed the finishing pierce. If this internal restraint occurred, he would have wondered incessantly what caused it. Remembrance of that shortcoming and the fate it left him prey to would have brought on anxiety enough to make him despair of his courage and sufficiency in self-defense.

> There's a divinity that shapes our ends,
> Rough-hew them how we may.

What did the Lord have against him? No, it was impossible that the darling of the gods should be abandoned thus and cast aside like carrion. No, the cause of his defeat lurked somewhere beyond God's design, not in the stars nor in the fabric of his being, but in sheer malice, the treachery of quiet possession by quintessential evil—the Devil, in short. The peril of our poet when he set to work on Hamlet was spiritual: he wrote for the salvation of his soul from terror of the Prince of Darkness and hell, who had by some unknown invitation made his residence therein.

By the same crude method which accounted for his failure in the Knyvet affair, De Vere explained his neglect of revenge for Leycester's victory over Sussex. He simply could not strike at the "bloody bawdy villain" because Leycester had swarms of friends and servants around him. The Queen connived on his side. And the Fiend—in concord with the Puritan sect—held

Robin Dudley dear. What could poor Oxford do? It was his duty to do something: a feat of singular merit, Vere-like, great. He wrote the tragical history of the Prince of Denmark.

Someone whispered to the Queen in June 1583 that Leycester and his countess Lettice, whom he had secretly married under a cloud of slanders after the death in Ireland of her warlord Walter Devereux, Earl of Essex, were planning to win King James of Scotland as a son-in-law. They wanted the Scotch monarch, whose lovedreams leaned him toward Platonic pederasty, to take for his bride one of Dudley's stepdaughters. When Elizabeth heard of the design to make a Devereux girl a queen, she became angrier than the bruit ever made her that charged her darling Earl with arranging the death of his Amy Robsart by a fall down a staircase and the death of the Earl of Essex by Italian poisoning. "If there was a person in the world Elizabeth loathed it was the woman who had dared to become the wife of the only man she had thought of seriously for herself. She was in such a fury when she heard (of Letitia's plot to be James's mother-in-law) that she said she would rather see James stripped of his crown than wedded to that she-wolf's cub."[64] De Vere's reflections on the affair helped him to compose *Hamlet.*

A

I imagine that *Hamlet* was given a trial performance in the summer of 1584, and after a scrutiny of the public's response some mystifying alterations were made, to confuse the onlookers who detected in the drama the features and expressions of individuals prominent in the state. Gradually Shakespeare transformed the play from a melodrama of imperial government to a lyrical tragedy of family life

It may have been under the spell of *Hamlet* that a riot broke out in Shoreditch in June 1584. A mob of apprentices round the Theater and the Curtain battled students from the Inns of Court. The fray recalls the collision of Oxford's servants with the law students and Thomas Knyvet's men, but it could have been the last outburst of Sussex antagonism to Leycester's legal stalwarts. The Mayor of London blamed the plays. He begged the Privy Council to suppress them and demolish the two offending playhouses. All the Councilors agreed to silence the players except the Lord Chamberlain Charles Howard and Vice-Chamberlain Christopher Hatton. The City Recorder sent for the Queen's company and the Earl of Arundel's actors to compel them to stop acting; they obeyed. He sent next for the owner of the Theater, but stubborn James Burbage replied that he was Lord Hunsdon's man and would not come. A sheriff's deputy had to bring him in. Old James had started his theatrical career as a servant of the Earl of Leycester. Entering the service of Henry Carey, Lord Hunsdon, he became occasionally a puppet in the politics of Sussex, to whom Hunsdon stanchly adhered. I suspect that Oxford, who had been a cavalry companion of Hunsdon in the 1570 expedition headed by Sussex to the Scottish border, took a hand in Burbage's change of masters, but we are ignorant of the time and circumstances of the change. It did not draw the obscene attention that the brothers John and Laurence Dutton drew when, in March 1580, they led the actors of the Earl of Warwick, Leycester's brother, into the service of De Vere. The guess has been offered that Burbage donned the livery of Hunsdon about March 1583, when the chief comedians of Leycester's troop were employed by the Master of the Revels for the newly formed Queen's company. When Henry Carey was appointed Chamberlain of the royal household in 1585 Burbage and his troop were enlisted as the Lord Chamberlain's players, in which company his son Richard shone as the star. Richard, you know, won his fame chiefly in performance of William Shakespeare's plays, *Hamlet* above all.

The earliest sign of the drama's impact that I have come across is in Robert Greene's pamphlet romance *Arbasto; The*

Anatomy of Fortune, which the publisher registered on August 13, 1584. The protagonist of this tale is a king of Denmark, tho there is nothing Danish in the story or its scenes. King Arbasto has a brother Tebaldo who sojourns, like Laertes, "in France, as one desirous to see the manners of strange countries, and to furnish himself with all the qualities fit for a worthy gentleman." When Tebaldo is killed at the French court, the Danish monarch swears revenge and invades France. He wins several battles and meets the princess Doralicia, who (like Ophelia) is "beautified"—but with the gifts of nature rather than those of art. The Dane wishes to slay her father but is captured and kept behind bars while his army is massacred. Her sister Myrania helps him escape; they fly to Denmark where he summons a parliament and gains their approval of his marriage to the French traitress. Then she discovers his passion for Doralicia and in despair she dies, prophesying: "after my death my ghost shall torment him with ghastly visions." Arbasto declares that if his comrade Egerio and others had not restrained him—"I had sent my soul with hers to the grave." Egerio conspires with some nobles to seize the crown for himself. The king eludes them and sails away to the Mediterranean, where he enters a new career—as a priest of the goddess Astarte! *Arbasto, King of Denmark*, as the novelette came to be titled, is just the sort of romance a speedy writer like Greene would have concocted in a fortnight out of old Hellenic plots and episodes, and reminiscences from the primary *Hamlet*.

In May 1585 the Lord Chamberlain Charles Howard was appointed Admiral of the English navy. Edward Alleyn, the most popular actor of the epoch, organized a troop of players for the Admiral. The new troop worked at first in a kind of partnership with Hunsdon's, now the Lord Chamberlain's men. A modern researcher, without any concern for the Looney theory of Shakespearean authorship, arrived at a curious judgment on the development of these two companies. "Surprising as it may appear," he states, "the facts lead to the conclusion that, when Alleyn joined Burbage in 1585, taking with him men from Worcester's and Sheffield's companies, to form the Admiral's company, he, with his brother John Alleyn, Robert Browne, and Richard Jones, combined the remainder, or part of the remainder of the two companies with Oxford's company; this amalgamation working under Oxford's title in summer at the Curtain, and probably at the Boar's Head in winter, until 1589, in which year Oxford's company disappears from all theatrical records, not appearing again for thirteen years, and then appearing, united and performing with Worcester's men at the Curtain and the Boar's Head."[65] The researcher was unacquainted with the fact that the residence of the Alleyn brothers stood next door to a gorgeous mansion occupied by Oxford and the artists who served him—"his lewd friends," in Burghley's phrase. From his house the Earl—commonly designated the Lord Chamberlain—supervised the tragedians and the comedians of the city.[65a] He was the master-mind who arranged for the Admiral's servants and the Chamberlain's troop to act together before the Queen at Greenwich palace on January 6, 1586. The drama that implored their joint exertions this night, I surmise, was *Hamlet*. It probably appealed to Burghley as a moral lesson, demonstrating the truth of his utterance of November 1584: "The desire of sovereignty is so great that no device could bridle ambitious minds."[66]

In October 1585 Lord Willoughby had gone to Denmark again, this time in the hope of obtaining military assistance for King Henry of Navarre, who was fighting to make France safe for Protestants. King Frederick welcomed the ambassador warmly and proposed to feast him all winter, "with no lack of Rhenish wine." The Dane carried Queen Elizabeth's picture in a tablet of gold near his heart. But he grudged her the many soldiers she wanted for Navarre, chagrined because she had not sent him aid in his recent war with the Swedes. From Denmark Oxford's brother-in-law journeyed to Holland where he took a place in the English army commanded by the Earl of Leycester. We know how Oxford had desired the generalship of this army. He managed to win from her Majesty the assignment of Master of the Horse. But Leycester would not stand for his rival commanding the cavalry. After less than a month of glory and felicity in the Low Countries, Oxford had to withdraw and sail home. The upshot of this experience, and his ensuing meditations on the factional jealousy and fighting among the English officers, was *Othello, the Moor of Venice.*[67] A specialist on the Tudor theater noted that *Othello* bears evidence of having been written with phrases from the first quarto of *Hamlet* ringing in the writer's brain.[68]

One of Oxford's former intimates, Rowland York—the man who had played Iago to his Desdemona—was granted by Leycester the post of governor in Zutphen. York sold the citadel o Spain, claiming that he could not endure to bear arms any more under the banner of heresy. He declared himself a devout Catholic. But the Spaniards did not trust him with any important army office. He died in the beginning of 1588 with agonizing symptoms of syphilis. It is not beyond the bounds of possibility that Shakespeare named the court fool of King Hamlet after this gallant York. In the course of Chapter E I will show why.

Oxford's sister Mary had a baby daughter in May 1586 and she wished to name her Sophia, after the Danish queen. Her husband insisted that the child be christened Katherine, in memory of his mother, and Katherine Bertie she was baptized. Her uncle Edward was of course among the Earls that attended the banquet afterward in Willoughby House.

In this merry month of May William Kemp, the chief clown of Leycester's company, and seven other actors traveled to Elsinore to amuse the Danes with music and acrobatics. After some months in King Frederick's service they went down to Germany, but were back in England before Christmas

1587, when Leycester's troop entertained the Court for the last time.

The year 1587 found the theaters of London busy as beehives. A government observer regretted that they were so prosperous, because he blamed on them the emptiness of the churches. "Every day in the week," he affirmed, "the players' bills are set up in sundry places of the city, some in the name of her Majesty's men, some the Earl of Leycester's, some the Earl of Oxford's, the Lord Admiral's, and divers others," so that when the bells clamored for sermons the trumpets sounded for plays—"whereat the wicked faction of Rome laugheth for joy."[69] There is no sign of any performance of *Hamlet* in this year.

In December the dramatist's father-in-law sent him a letter which reminds us of Hamlet's declaration, "I lack advancement." It appears in the first quarto in the form: "I want preferment." Burghley said, "You seem to infer that the lack of your preferment cometh of me, for that you could never hear of any way prepared for your preferment. My Lord, for a direct answer, I affirm for a truth—and it to be well proved—that your Lordship mistaketh my power." Burghley refrained from indicating the men whom he called "hinderers" of Oxford's political progress.[70] But the Earl persisted in believing that Cecil used his influence only to advance the Cecils, and thought of his son-in-law just like King Claudius, "with wisest sorrow…Together with remembrance of ourselves." Shakespeare unveiled the Lord Treasurer's egotism in the speech of Polonius counseling his son, "To thine own self be true…"

February 1588 commenced a series of historic solemnities, griefs and trifles which must have revived in our poet's head his sufferings and associations prior to the writing of *Hamlet*. First came the news of the death of his former comrade, Rowland York, the traitor—a victim, they said, either of Spanish poison or the French pox. Next, on March 9, Frances Radcliff, the widow of Sussex, died. Nothing of note seems to have happened on the anniversary of Julius Caesar's murder. A pamphlet was issued about this time on "A Battle Fought in Poland" by the Swedes against the Poles on Christmas day the year before. Frederick II of Denmark died on April 4, only thirty years old: the age of Shakespeare's prince at the time of his death. Christian IV was elected king of the Danes. Oxford's birthday fell on April 12. Reviewing his 38 years, he would surely have felt sad. His life appeared a spectacle of wasted genius, humiliating especially in the domains of arms and art—the courtier, soldier, scholar, quite overthrown.

Early in May the rumor reached London that the king of Sweden had been killed by one of his companions and his crown prince thrust in prison. There was also talk about Maurice of Nassau, the young warlord of the Dutch, described by Lord Willoughby as "hot-headed, coveting honor," and ambitious to marry a princess of Denmark. Willoughby was confident that Maurice would make a fine instrument of English policy: "He might be catched and kept in a fish-pool," he told Burghley, "while in his imagination he may judge it a sea."[71] This metaphor may have come to Shakespeare's eye and inspired the whimsical affirmation of Hamlet, "I could be bounded in a nutshell and count myself king of infinite space…" De Vere's brother-in-law had succeeded Leycester as the chief general of the English in the Low Countries. He proved the better soldier by far. For his guide and philosopher in warfare Bertie took Francois de la Nour, the great Huguenot veteran, popularly loved as Bras de Fer—Iron Arm—because he had lost his left arm in battle and wore a metal one in its place. Bras de Fer's *Politic and Military Discourses* had been published in English in 1588. It is likely that his nickname gave Shakespeare the idea of naming his Norwegian prince like a Frenchman, Fortinbras (Strong Arm).

On Thursday, June 5, 1588 the heartsick Countess of Oxford died of a fever at Greenwich palace, leaving her fourth daughter just one year old. Her father's sorrow was exorbitant and dismayed his friends. On the 8th the Queen gave De Vere the consolation of a grant of Earls Colne Priory, the burial building of so many of his ancestors; but Anne De Vere was not buried there. Her funeral took place in Westminster Abbey on June 25. A host of mourners, including Lady Mary Vere Bertie, followed the Countess to her grave. Her husband could not be present.

Edward seems to have gone to sea, to assist his friend Admiral Howard in the battle against the Spanish Armada. Unfortunately he missed the main fight. Returning to the land he restlessly rode on July 27 to the camp of the army at Tilbury, where Leycester held command. "I trust he be free," Dudley wrote to Walsingham, "to go to the enemy, for he seems most willing to hazard his life in this quarrel." Elizabeth however was desirous that the wayward Earl should have the government of the strategic port of Harwich. "My Lord," said Leycester, "seemed at the first to like well of it. Afterward he came to me and told me he thought the place of no service nor credit." So he went to her Majesty with a request for a nobler job, and Robin his rival confessed he was "gladder to be rid of him than to have him."[71a] The weary Leycester had seen the last of his enemy, for he died on September 4. Within the month his players disbanded and Will Kemp, George Bryan and Thomas Pope joined the servants of Lord Strange, who merged eventually with the Chamberlain's men.

The top comedian of the period, Dick Tarlton, was buried on September 3. Among the daring jokes Tarlton was famed for, one stands out as a fulfillment of the prophecy that Walter Ralegh made about Oxford's gratitude to him. The Earl instigated the clown to lift his finger in Ralegh's direction during a play when he had to recite the sentence, "The knave commands the queen."[72] The anecdote shows us how faithful the supreme comedian was to the interests of De Vere, reflecting the loyalty of a host of historionic workingmen. Incidentally, I do not believe that Shakespeare burlesqued Ralegh in the character of Osric. More typical than individual, Osric may stand for any rich ass in the Elizabethan court. In the first quarto he is designated simply "A Braggart Gentleman."

A trivial note in the English government accounts of military expenses in the Low Countries this year suggests where Shakespeare got the curious name of Yaughan for the person who supplies his gravedigging clowns with liquor (Act V, Scene 1). The note reports a sum of money due a Dutch widow of Flushing named Yoghan for victuals she supplied to English soldiers. Oxford's kinsmen riding under the Dutch flag would have told him salty anecdotes about her.

In the summer of 1587 Thomas Kyd entered the employment of the mysterious Lord for whose players Christopher Marlowe and other artists worked. Thomas Watson, who had dedicated a hundred love sonnets to Oxford in 1582, apparently also wrote plays for this unknown nobleman. He and Marlowe were close collaborators in this period. At the same time Marlowe did secret service for the government and in October carried messages for the Lord Treasurer. Another playwright, Anthony Munday, called himself a "Messenger of her Majesty's Chamber" in the romance of *Palmerin d'Olivia* which he delivered to the press in January 1588, dedicated to De Vere. The most exciting drama performed in these months was Marlowe's *Tamburlaine*, acted by the Admiral's men. Imitations of this epic were numerous, but one merits a passing glance here, the lost *History of George Scanderbeg*, whose sole official record states that it was acted by the Earl of Oxford's company. Gabriel Harvey alludes to the play in mocking Marlowe's friend Thomas Nash, and calls Nash "the Scanderbegging wight." This means, I take it, Nash wrote that epic or else was regarded as the writer. If so, then we have here a clew to the identity of the unknown Lord to whom Nash refers in his works as the master with whom he traveled in the country and served in obscure literary ways.

Charles Wisner Barrell has demonstrated that Nash's lord is the same man the funny young scholar hailed as "Gentle Master William"—"the most copious Carminist (i.e. song-maker) of our time."[73] Nash's description fits no man but Edward de Vere. The Earl was willing to be known merely as Will in his capacities as a pastoral poet and composer of comedies. (See Thalia in Edmund Spenser's *Tears of the Muses.*) When he came to tragedy he shrouded himself at first in complete anonymity. Nevertheless, I am convinced that Nash, for one, had a fair idea who the "English Seneca" was.

The reference of Nash to Hamlet in Robert Greene's *Menaphon* suggests that the Prince of Denmark was a familiar hero in England prior to August 23, 1589, when *Menaphon* was licensed for printing. Early this year, in my opinion, perhaps in March again, Shakespeare worked on his tragedy of the Dane. Then, after some cutting and condensing, an unknown company staged *Hamlet* in a form approximating the quarto of 1603.

The revision abolished the external obstacles to the Prince's revenge and made his delay the result of his doubt of the Ghost, and the practical difficulties of his test-play, and the departure to England. What Hamlet lost in muscular adolescent cleverness, he gained in intellectual stature, in maturity. He improved in eloquence too, with "handfuls of tragical speeches." The religion of the Prince received a new emphasis: his soliloquy on the alternatives of action and submission became an utterance of his faith in divine justice after death, a confidence which is absent in the later text. When the Hamlet of the 1603 play dies, his last words are a prayer that heaven would receive his soul.

The Prince's problem was now adroitly contrasted with the family loyalties of Laertes and Fortinbras. The personality of the latter became clearer and more vital to the plot as the one destined to set right the disjointed Danish state. In the figure of this warlike savior Shakespeare painted an idealized sketch of King James of Scotland, whose marriage with Anne of Denmark was warmly rumored in January 1589. The poet apparently conceived him as a son seeking not vengeance for the judicial murder of his mother, but the healing of the wounds of his kingdom, and the kingdom to the south. In January the news went to Germany, Queen Elizabeth had "declared that she appoints the King of Scots successor to the throne on her death."[74] Shakespeare approved. Hence the prophetic soul of Hamlet informed his countrymen, as the second quarto put it:

> I cannot live to hear the news from England,
> But I do prophesy the election lights
> On Fortinbras: he has my dying voice.

Horatio tells the northern prince that this prediction "will draw on more" to vote for him.

A more important alteration took place in the portrayal of Ophelia. She no longer played the role of a meretricious marionette of her father. All that remained of that portrayal was the lewdness of Hamlet aimed primarily at his mother, when Queen Gertrude invites him to sit by her: "No, good mother, here's metal more attractive." (Act III, Scene 2) The Earl of Oxford stands out among English thinkers by the glow of his cordial interest in the advances of science, in particular the chemistry of Paracelsus. Hamlet's joke on the magnetism of Ophelia plainly alluded to a book that came out in 1581, *The New Attractive*, containing a short discourse of the Magnes or Lodestone...Now first found out by Robert Norman, Hydrographer. De Vere's interest in the subject endured to his death. Four years before that grievous event Dr William Gilbert of Colchester, Essex, published his classic work *De Magnete*, where the word "electricity" first appeared. Hamlet's jest on the miner allure of Ophelia was intended to stir up his mother's jealousy. His remarks to he former concerning "country matters" only mirror the Prince's feelings of attraction and repulsion in the atmosphere of venery pervading the summit of the state. The aggression thus exhibited to the girl represents an effort to shake off the spell of her chastity as well as a testimonial of madness.

In primrose ambience the virgin walks, a little miracle of white pathos, and Hamlet assures her and the universe—and so himself—that he truly loved her once. Ophelia evolved into a victim of paternal craft, keenly intelligent about pastors who permit themselves touches of depravity, while her lover's character transformed into that of a victim of paternal brutality. The theme of the tragedy changed from the passion for fatherly sovrenty to the maltreatment of children for the sake of parental power.

Shakespeare's genius had not yet ripened to the point where it would show the world half-consciously what happened when fathers and mothers offended their sons and daughters sexually and imposed on them tasks of falsehood and bloodiness. In 1589 he was content with the bare discovery that the thing rotten in the state of "Denmark" was the moral autocracy in the family. The principle of Hamlet at this stage may be stated in the language of a pamphlet (alleged to be by Nash) issued against the Puritans in the following year: "As then the government of common-weals was first drawn from the government of private houses, so that which is the ruin of private houses grows in time to be the ruin of common-weals."[75]

B

The preface to Greene's *Menaphon* in which Nash spoke of Hamlet provides us with other fragments of vivacious information about the English theater. After deriding the plagiarism of Thomas Kyd and praising the ingenuity of George Peele, he goes on to laughter at the actors for their disregard of debt to the playwrights: "Sundry other sweet gentlemen I do know, that have vaunted their pens in private devices, and tricked up a company of taffeta fools with their feathers, whose beauty, if our poets had not pieced with the supply of their periwigs, they might have anticked it until this time up and down the country with The King of Fairies, and dined every day at the pease-porridge ordinary with Delfrigus." These gentlemen to whose brains Nash attributes the graces of the theaters are referred to affectionately by Edmund Spenser in the sonnet to De Vere which he composed for *The Fairy Queen* (licensed for publication on December 1, 1589). Spenser wrote that he esteemed the Earl for "The antique glory of thine ancestry," and

> thine own long living memory,
> Succeeding them in true nobility,
> And also for the love which thou dost bear
> To the 'Heliconian imps', and they to thee,
> They unto thee, and thou to them most dear.

The expression "Heliconian imps" is probably a quotation from Oxford himself. The "imps" were those devilish advocates of the Muses whom Burghley despises as the Earl's "lewd friends, who still rule him by flatteries."[76]

Altho Cecil despised the playwrights, he appreciated the players for their labors in the cause of patriotism and the war propaganda against Spain. In 1589 the Lord Treasurer sent his usher Walter Cope to request that the money-lender John Hyde should hand over to Cuthbert Burbage the keys of the Theater, which Hyde had locked up for a mortgage. Cuthbert brought Hyde the money for payment of the mortgage in full, but where he got the money, nobody knows. Certainly not from Burghley. Perhaps from his son-in-law, whom the Queen had granted a thousand pounds a year from her secret-service treasury.

In this year 1589 the singing boys of St Paul's Cathedral, directed by John Lyly, the Earl's secretary, got into trouble with the government because of their boldness in staging satire on the Puritans. For bringing religious debate into the theater, the company was forced to dissolve. They performed at Court for the last time on January 6, 1590. Spenser deplored their loss in the *Tears of the Muses*. He presented Thalia, the muse of comedy, weeping over the disappearance from the London scene of the wondrous "Willy," their chief dramatist.

Where be the sweet delights of learnings treasure,
That wont with Comic sock to beautify
The painted Theaters, and fill with pleasure
The listeners eyes, and ears with melody;
In which I late was wont to rain as Queen,
And mask in mirth with Graces well beseen?

O all is gone, and all that goodly glee,
Which wont to be the glory of gay wits
Is laid abed, and nowhere now to see;
And in her room unseemly Sorrow sits,
With hollow brows and grisly countenance,
Marring my joyous gentle dalliance...

All places they with folly have possest,
And with vain toys the vulgar entertaine...

And he, the man, whom Nature's self had made
To mock her self, and Truth to imitate,
With kindly counter under Mimic shade,
Our pleasant Willy, ah, is dead of late:
With whom all joy and jolly merriment
Is also deaded, and in dolour drent.

In stead thereof scoffing Scurrility,
And scornful Folly with Contempt is crept,
Rolling in rimes of shameless ribaldry…

But that same gentle Spirit, from whose pen
Large Streams of honey and sweet Nectar flow,
Scorning the boldness of such base-born men,
Which dare their follies forth so rashly throw,
Doth rather choose to sit in idle Cell,
Than so himself to mockery to sell.

As late as November 9, 1595, the bruit trickled wherever courtiers and other nosers of news and devourers of intelligence congregated, "Some say my Lord of Oxford is dead."[76a] John Dryden and critics of his caliber affirmed that this Willy could be none other than our William Shakespeare; but the orthodoxy of Stratford on Avon rejected their belief, since it clashed with the chronology of Shakespeare's plays defended by that shrine. I need not repeat here Looney's argument that the Willy of Spenser's "Tears" is the very same Willie who sings comic verse in Spenser's *Shepherds Calendar* (1579). The latter, Looney proved, is none other than Edward of Oxford. The Earl was reputed among contemporary lovers of literature as a writer of superlative comic plays. He merited, according to the anonymous *Art of English Poesy* (1589), "the highest prize" for comedy and interlude. By the end of 1589, however, Oxford seems to have cut the connection between his name and dramatic creation. Official attacks on the freedom of the stage had a little to do with his decision. In October the Lord Mayor of London and his cronies protested to the Privy Council that the actors had become too "riotous." Some farces performed by the Admiral's men and Strange's company aroused the "utter dislike" of the city authorities and they obtained a letter from Burghley forbidding these troops to act in town. On November 6 Ned Alleyn and his fellows obeyed the decree. Strange's troop, on the contrary—now headed by the Burbages, who left the livery of Lord Hunsdon early this year—went away from the Mayor in "very contemptuous manner" and played that afternoon at the Cross Keys inn. He put two of them in jail. The Privy Council, indignant that "the players take upon themselves to handle in their plays certain matters of divinity and of state unfit to be suffered," established a censorship which Britain has endured to the present day. Shakespeare alludes to it in his sonnet with the lament about "art made tongue-tied by authority."

In 1590 four or five players who had worn Oxford's motley parted from the Admiral's troop, kissed London goodby and traveled across the Channel to cajole guilders from the Dutch with their comedies, chronicles, and athletic feats. When they made the same trip in 1591 they carried a letter from Admiral Howard which gives their names: Robert Browne, Richard Jones, John Bradstreet, Thomas Sackfield. The name of Robert Browne turns up later in a document by Oxford's daughter Elizabeth mentioning him as an actor beloved by her husband, William Stanley the Earl of Derby. Browne and his companions, most likely, introduced the works of Shakespeare to continental Europe. In producing *Hamlet* they probably made a cross-compromise between the versions of 1584 and 1589, which survives in distorted form in the German *Hamlet* we have reviewed.

February 1591 furnishes us with a cheerful glimpse of William Cecil's character both in office and at home. Roger Manners wrote to his brother John that Burghley was agreeable to take John's son into his service, but "the best he could do for him was to give him good counsel." Many boys have since had to learn by heart the substance of that counsel in Polonius's bleak blank verse.

Toward the close of 1591 the Earl of Oxford married his second wife, the Maid of Honor Elizabeth Trentham, who was distinguished for her beauty, the fortune she inherited, and courage extraordinary in her sex. One outcome of this marriage appears to have been the dialog that our poet added to the dumb-show in *Hamlet*, thereby weakening its impact on the King. (Claudius "blenches" but does not "unkennel" his guilt.) The dialog is mainly concerned with the too voluble avowals of the Duchess Baptista that she would love her first husband to her death. "None wed the second," she insists, "but who killed the first."

> The instances that second marriage move
> Are base aspects of thrift, but none of love;
> A second time I kill my husband dead,
> When second husband kisses me in bed.

I interpret these lines as a challenge of the dramatist's conscience inquiring into his motives for wedding Elizabeth Trentham. He did not marry her because he needed a housekeeper or a mother for his children. His three daughters were all cared for from infancy by nurses whom their grandfather William Cecil hired. Affection, the Earl unquestionably felt for his bride, who clearly pitied and adored him. But love? He wondered, he searched his heart for a fair answer, troubled by knowledge of his secret distrust and detestation of her sex. Beyond the shadow of a doubt, he felt that mentally (by the might of his thought) he had slain his first wife. Therefore he made Hamlet murmur, on listening to these lines, "Wormwood, wormwood." Overtly designed to gall Queen Gertrude, they have no emotional effect on her at all. They are bitter to nobody but the poet himself.

On December 2, 1591—before his marriage—Oxford alienated Castle Hedingham to Burghley and his three orphan girls. Perhaps this was the price the older man exacted for his consent to Oxford's taking a second wife. There is no testimony that the Earl ever saw his old home again. Elizabeth Trentham considered the loss an injury to the House of Vere.

She strove to recover the castle after her husband's death, for the good of her son, Earl Henry, and she did.

Earl Edward gave up the game of courtier and settled with his Countess in the suburb of Stoke Newington, near the playhouse where the Admiral's servants and the Chamberlain's men acted *Hamlet* on June 8, 1594. This Chamberlain's company had been recently organized, round the nucleus of Lord Strange's troop. Strange became the Earl of Derby in September 1593 and the troop was called by his new title until April 1594 when he died. His brother William Stanley succeeded to the earldom and married Elizabeth Vere. But he did not take over the patronage of the Derby players. In May they obtained the status of servants with Henry Carey, the Chamberlain of the Queen.

The company included the enigmatic talent of William Shakspere of Stratford on Avon, whose name appears in the records of the troop this year. No one knows when Shakspere, the son of a butcher, glover and sterquinarian, became a member. Some time after the christening of his twins Hamnet and Judith in February 1585, he went to London to look for a job. The next we know of him (apart from a vague assertion by his father that in 1587 he had concurred in a Warwickshire trade in real estate) is that in 1592 he had enough funds to lend one John Clayton seven pounds in Cheapside, and enough theatrical fame to prompt a sneer from the scribbler of Greene's *Groatsworth of Wit* against his practice of usury and his pretense to literary skill. (Greene did not write the *Groatsworth*; the evidence of the text preponderantly indicates Henry Chettle as the culprit author.) A tradition of Shakspere's family holds that he earned his first fellowship in a cry of players by attracting the good-will of an unknown gentleman who rescued him from the wages of horse-holding at the door of a theater.[77]

That Shakspere's benefactor and master was the Lord Chamberlain of England, you will readily understand when you see the affirmation of Robert Armin, the clown of the Chamberlain's company, about his own instructor and lord. "I take my journey," Armin wrote in December 1599, "(to wait on the right honourable good Lord, my Master whom I serve) to Hackney."[78] Hackney was the village outside London where the Earl of Oxford moved in 1596, a short distance for a horse to his beloved theaters. He resided there, at "King's Place," until his death in June 1604. Robert Armin took the place of William Kemp as the head jester of Shakespeare's company. Kemp's habit of interrupting dialog with impromptu buffoonery displeased his master and early in 1599 he was fired. The dramatist interrupted the action of *Hamlet* to criticize clowns like Kemp: "And let those that play your clowns speak no more than is set down for them; for there be of them that will themselves laugh, to set on some quantity of barren spectators to laugh too, though in the mean time some necessary question of the play be then to be considered; that's villainous, and shows a most pitiful ambition in the fool that uses it." There is no comedian in "The Murder of Gonzago." Shakespeare interjected the speech for a personal grievance, tired of watching comedians play havoc with his work.

When he wrote his critique of the improvising fools, the performance of plays by a certain troop of children was a "late innovation." It is generally agreed that he had in view the Children of the Chapel Royal, who acted for her Majesty and the Court on January 6, 1601, for the first time since February 1584. These "little eyases" (unfledged hawks)—no longer directed by a choirmaster but by profiteers—were drawing crowds to their roofed and restricted city theater, the Blackfriars, and enrapturing them with their earnest ingenuity. These crowds had more money and better manners than the public that flocked to the elder, sun-bleached weather-beaten stages. The Globe playhouse, where the Chamberlain's servants performed, lost business. Presumably Shakespeare was thinking of this when he made Rosenkrantz say that the child-actors were carrying off "Hercules and his load too." The flag of the Globe displayed the Greek hero bearing the world on his back. The allusion to Hercules is particularly interesting in the light of Hamlet's comparison of that hero with himself. (Act I, Scene 2; Act V, Scene 1)

The Prince delivers a gentle warning to the directors of the Chapel choir-boys that "their writers do them wrong, to make them exclaim" in derision of the adult actors. Hamlet's admonition helps us to date the final revision of the play. On September 2, 1600 Henry Evans leased the Blackfriars from Richard Burbage and started producing plays with the Chapel Royal children on September 29. Evans and his partners actually kidnapped little boys to sing and act on their stage. That accounts for Hamlet's curiosity about "the late innovation" and his interest in the infant actors' fate. One of the comedies Evans produced in the winter of 1600 was *Cynthia's Revels* by Ben Jonson, who put in the mouths of the children a number of sarcasms against the Chamberlain's men. Thus he made fun of the fact that "the umbrae or ghosts of some three or four plays, departed a dozen years since, have been seen walking on your stage here." He begged his audience to beware of such "hobgoblins" and singled out the "departed" play of *Hamlet* for his gayest barbs. "The dor, the dor…the palpable dor!" shouts a character observing a contest, mimicking Osric's "A hit, a palpable hit." We are shown a pageant of virgins in which "The fourth, in white, is Apheleia, a nymph as pure and simple as the soul, or as an abrase table, and is therefore called Simplicity…The word under her silver shield, Omnis abest fucus." Fucus is a kind of cosmetic; but Jonson obviously intended a slur on more than the nymph's face-paint. He recalled, I suppose, the profound predilection of Ophelia for genital jokes, or the scene of her drowning while she strained to pluck the long purple orchid, the phallic flower, "which liberal shepherds give a grosser name." The figure of Amorphus in *Cynthia's Revels* appears to be a caricature of

Hamlet or Hamlet's creator: he is a gentleman "so alone in fashion; able to render the face of any statesman living;" and he exhibits a marked fondness for "a dish of sliced caviar."

If Shakespeare put the last touches on the Prince of Denmark after the novelty of the Chapel enterprise, it is conceivable that he began writing the second quarto text on Saint Patrick's day, 1601. His changes on this occasion rendered the drama conscious self-portraiture.

In the course of exploring his interior self, he returned in a sense to the theme he had set forth in the primary version of the play. Instead of the positive passion for tyranny, he now laid stress on the negative impulse of rebellion against the parental will. Hamlet steadily declines to seek justice for his father's murder; he not only procrastinates, he forgets; and in his revolt turns criminal himself. The Prince of Denmark becomes in his pride an unconscious incarnation of Lucifer, the Prince of Darkness, resisting the authority of both his fathers and his mother with the most subtle militancy, flaunting only his irreverence. The motto of Hamlet might well be a contradiction of the Prince of Wales' Ich dien nicht. Even when he attempts constructive criticism, he renders it with infernal warmth. He commands the players to reform their histrionics "altogether." He attacks the drinking practice of his country as "a custom more honored in the breach than in the observance." His cure for marital fault and vice is abstinence— "I say, we will have no more marriages." So excessive are his virtue and idealism that their enmity to the human peers out unaware. The super-Christian shows himself a second Satan, an adversary of mankind and indeed all life. "Things rank and gross in nature," he contends, "Possess it merely." The friend of Horatio puts his misanthropic conviction mildly when he says, "Man delights me not; no, nor woman neither." All the uses of this world are repellent to him.

In polar opposition to him stands Fortinbras, the son who fulfills his father's testament. When Shakespeare imagined the troops of Fortinbras on the march to Poland, he may have been remembering the great battle of Nieuport fought in the Netherlands on July 2, 1600. The English soldiers at this fight, led by Francis and Horace Vere, did feats of savage valor against the army of Spain that merited the immortality of Shakespeare's pen. "It was a hot struggle of twenty thousand men, pent up in a narrow space, where the very nature of the ground had made artistic evolutions nearly impracticable. The advance, the battalia, even the rearguard on both sides were mixed together pell-mell, and the downs were soon covered at every step with the dead and dying—Briton, Hollander, Spaniard, Italian, Frisian, Frenchman, Walloon, fighting and falling together, and hotly contesting every inch of those barren sands."[79] Sir Francis Vere was shot twice and forced to retire, since Prince Maurice did not send him aid in time. His brother Horace headed a splendid charge that broke the enemy's resistance, and the little territory of the struggle was once more Holland's own. "This was a bloody morsel that we strove for," wrote Sir Francis afterward.[80] When we read the account of this battle over a strip of barren sand, we cannot help recalling the lines of Hamlet extolling Prince Fortinbras and his soldiers while they march "to gain a little patch of ground."

> Witness this army of such mass and charge,
> Led by a delicate and tender Prince,
> Whose spirit with divine ambition puft
> Makes mouths at the invisible event,
> Exposing what is mortal, and unsure,
> To all that fortune, death, or danger dare…
> for a fantasy and trick of fame
> Go to their graves like beds, fight for a plot
> Whereon the numbers cannot try the cause,
> Which is not tomb enough and continent
> To hide the slain.

The truth is that Hamlet has no knowledge of the numbers that would try the cause of Fortinbras in Poland. The price of honor here, he imagines, is "The imminent death of twenty thousand men"—the very number involved in the battle of Nieuport.

The Dane envies the destructive energy of the Prince of Norway because it burns with creative purpose, the restoration and extension of his family's imperial authority. Realising what a wretched monarch he himself would make, Hamlet has nothing to live for.

> But why should he,
> The expectancy and rose of the fair state,
> The glass of fashion and the mold of form,
> The observ'd of all observers,

be so deject and wretched, capable of unpacking his heart with nothing but words or sinister deeds? What was it that upset his "noble and most sovereign reasons" and downed it to the function of a court fool? "Your only jig-maker." Revising the tragedy for the last time, our dramatist fought a magnificent struggle to understand himself in the person of his darling prince. He relinquished his former religious explanations. No harsh duty to God nor lure of the Devil was to blame. Shakespeare indeed was now a disciple of the Greek skeptics. He granted Sextus Empiricus the homage he had once paid the stoics of Rome. The genius of Nicholas Hill, the father of atomic philosophy in England, had something to do with the change. Hill served the Earl of Oxford as secretary in the dramatist's old age. So Hamlet still sang of heaven and hell, but confessed that he had no certainty about the dreams that might follow after death. He could now conceive of circumstances in which "sweet religion" might be looked on as just "a rhapsody of words." On the threshold of his own extinction he utters not a word of piety: "The rest is silence." As for his pursuit of the truth concerning his life's frustration, the essence of his errors, here was the new wisdom he had acquired:

> So, oft it chances in particular men,
> That for some vicious mole of nature in them,
> As in their birth—wherein they are not guilty,
> Since nature cannot choose his origin—
> By the o'ergrowth of some complexion,
> Oft breaking down the pales and forts of reason,
> Or by some habit that too much o'erleavens
> The form of plausive manners; that those men,
> Carrying, I say, the stamp of one defect,
> Being nature's livery, or fortune's star,
> Their virtues else, be they as pure as grace,
> As infinite as man may undergo,
> Shall in the general censure take corruption
> From that particular fault. The dram of e'il (evil, ill)
> Doth all the noble substance oft adulter
> To his own scandal.

Hamlet is provoked to this speech by the superflux of wine he sees drunk by King Claudius and his courtiers. The subject was a painful one for the Earl of Oxford. His outbreak against Lord Harry Howard and Charles Arundel followed a warning they gave him in July 1580 that he should refrain from wild drinking and loquacity among his cups.

In soliloquy after soliloquy Shakespeare tried to delineate the "mole of nature" or constellation of habit which had made his life so fantastic, enslaved him to passion and deprived him of manly tranquility. He tried to search out the source of his malady but could not succeed. His self-love, for one thing, would never allow him to face the naked truth. Dread of losing reason put barriers in its way. Perhaps he attempted the impossible. Nature may have provided the narcissic nucleus with a scotoma, a blind spot, precisely as she made one for the eye. Yet, I dare say, the poet touched the truth. In that very speech on physical endowment and fortune, it seems to me, he let slip the key to his mystery. It was something more elemental than he ever guessed, a baser matter of fact. The words in which I find the solution of his riddle are "vicious mole."

To the brain of the dramatist, with its boundless appetite for puns, "mole" meant not only a birthmark but the blind subterranean beast, and that animal in turn signified his protagonist's father. "Well said, old mole! Canst work i' the earth so fast?" So Hamlet questions the spirit of his father—"this fellow in the cellarage"—on learning that he cannot escape the Ghost, the demonic dictator of his lifework. He mocks the paternal fantom, calling him "mole": yet his ego submits to the government of the blind one underground. Shakespeare no longer had the Ghost exhort: "Vindicta! Revenge!" or (as Samuel Rowlands quotes him) "Hamlet, revenge my griefs." All the apparition ultimately wants is to be remembered. And Hamlet promises to throw everything else in his thought to oblivion.

Remember thee!

> Ay, thou poor ghost, while memory holds a seat
> In this distracted globe. Remember thee!
> Yea, from the table of my memory
> I'll wipe away all trivial fond records
> And saws of books, all forms, all pressures past,
> That youth and observation copied there;
> And thy commandment all alone shall live
> Within the book and volume of my brain…

Naturally the poet had no power to obliterate his cerebral store of education and experience. All he could do was endeavor to subject it, stock and lock, to the sway of the memory of his "mole." After that he might revolt and ridicule and bewail, as he pleased: he could never free his soul from the autocratic dead.

C

The apparition of King Hamlet, according to my theory, was created first of all in the image of Oxford's paternal protector Sussex. Stern soldiers and majestic statesmen both, they have scarcely a weakness to mark them human. The following praise of Thomas Radcliff illustrates how he excelled his fellow mortals: "Wise and loyal as Burghley, without his blind attachment to the monarch; vigilant as Walsingham, but disdaining his low cunning; magnificent as Leycester, but incapable of hypocrisy; and brave as Raleigh, with the piety of a primitive Christian: he seemed above the common objects of human ambition, and wanted, if the expression may be allowed, those dark shades of character which make men the heroes of history."[81] The sole defect I have been able to locate in the life of Sussex is the effort he made while a general in Ireland to bribe a servant of the rebel Shane O'Neill to poison his chief. But this sort of war-saving device had been advocated by no less a virtuous politician than Saint Thomas More.

Artists in literature have long deplored the impossibility of making a truly pure character a reality in fiction, convincing, red-blooded, like sin. Sussex dead rose up in our dramatist's imagination a god. He simply could not be staged except as a ghost. Hamlet compares his father to the sun titan Hyperion, and affirms that by his death the realm was divested of "Jove himself." He repeats this extolment to his mother: "See what a grace was seated on this brow: Hyperion's curls, the front of Jove himself…

> A combination and a form indeed
> Where every god did seem to set his seal,

"To give the world," he adds in what amounts to anticlimax, "assurance of a man."

By the way, the Prince's condemnation of the Queen for deserting Hyperion to marry a satyr echoes almost directly a lyric by the Earl of Oxford. His best-known poem laughs at women in exactly the same vein Hamlet uses to denounce them:

> To mark the choice they make, and how they change,
> How oft from Phoebus do they cleave to Pan.

"Frailty, thy name is woman," cries the Prince. "How frail those creatures are," sings the Earl in the same poem.

If the poet believed Lady Sussex an adulteress, he would have wished to believe also that her husband was clandestinely slain. The notorious booklet *Leycester's Commonwealth*, originally printed in Paris (by Charles Arundel and other fugitives) in the fall of 1584, suggested that the Lord Chamberlain had been poisoned: "The late Earl of Sussex...wanted not a scruple... of some dram received that made him incurable." Radcliff's Countess did not marry again. She put a permanent shield over her honor by the endowment of Sidney-Sussex College. And she died childless.

Queen Gertrude represents not only the Countess Frances but the Queen Elizabeth too. Our dramatist depicted her Majesty as Sussex's royal mistress in the political meaning of the term and as Leycester's mistress in the double sense. The royal caresses that Robert Dudley got maddened De Vere, who had once enjoyed the privilege of "love matters" with Elizabeth in 1573. In 1579, when Oxford nearly came to blows with Philip Sidney, the political adherents of Philip's uncle dared to dream in public that he would marry the Queen. Her favors intoxicated Leycester to the degree where he ventured to show his enmity to the Duke of Anjou, the candidate of France for the coronet of Elizabeth's consort. Lord Robert's attacks on the proposal for the French alliance angered her Majesty and she contemplated a scheme to cool him in the Tower. The magnanimous Sussex told her, "You must allow lovers their jealousy." Elizabeth relented, probably to Oxford's regret. His hatred of the favorite was increased by the gossip that Dudley had offered Anne Vavasor a hundred pounds a year in land rents, with many jewels, "for satisfying of his lusts."[82] This was only one of the reasons for which Oxford was alleged to have plotted the assassination of Leycester. How many times must the porches of his ears have been flushed with the lecherous lies that Charles Arundel told about Leycester, and inscribed with Thomas Fitzherbert in the notorious booklet they printed in Paris, 1584, *Discours de la Vie Abominable du Comte de Lecestre*? "He makes it his duty," they said, "to sow discord between great lords and their ladies…he made the gulf between the Earl of oxenford and his wife, daughter of Milord the Treasurer: and this for satisfaction of the untiring hate he bears for the Lord Treasurer."[82a] When he discovered how Charles Arundel and Henry Howard had fooled him, the real carvers of the gulf between him and his wife, his hatred of Leycester diminisht a little but never blew away. He even enjoyed slaying him in stage-effigy more than he lusted to kill his cousins Arundel and Howard in the persons of Rosencrantz and Guildenstern. Is it merely by chance that Shakespeare placed Earl Robert's nickname in the mouth of the mad Ophelia when he had her sing of her lost loves? "For bonny sweet Robin is all my joy."

In the last analysis the spirit of Queen Gertrude is the spirit of Countess Margaret Golding de Vere Tyrrell, as her son revived her in his fantasy. The contradictions in the Queen's personality are the result of conflict between the poet's desire to think that his mother really admired and loved him and his outrage at her failure to devote herself exclusively to his interest. The idea of incest obsesses Hamlet. Over and over again he calls the marriage of Claudius and his sister-in-law incestuous, tho Christendom had not agreed with Henry VIII that his marriage with his sister-in-law, Catherine of Aragon, had been a violation of divine law. Hamlet projects to the Ghost (who is silent to everybody else) his conviction that the Queen's chastity is mere seeming, that in fact she is a prostitute. Why? Because she married within a month or two of her first husband's death. Shakespeare was well aware that Sir or Saint Thomas More in 1511, within a month after his first wife's death, married the widow Middleton, and still kept the world's respect. The Church never considered More's dexterity in hasting to the widow's sheets a sin in any sense. The conscience of Hamlet, voiced by the Ghost, forbids him to crave revenge on his mother. No sooner is the Ghost gone than his ego blazes out, "O most pernicious woman!" The first object of his wrath is mother Gertrude, not the smiling villain, his stepfather. In his jealousy later he taunts the Queen with a pretense of caring more for the loveliness of Ophelia: "No, good mother, here's metal more attractive." When summoned to her Majesty's chamber, after exposing the guilt of Claudius to the satisfaction of himself and Horatio, he goes to her with urges to matricide in his heart. Under the caution of his ideal of princely dignity, he promises not to stab her to death:

> I will speak daggers to her, but use none.
> My tongue and soul in this be hypocrites.

In Gertrude's presence, inflated by a sentiment of sanctimony or righteousness, he accuses her of being an accomplice in his father's death. According to the quarto of 1603, "he throws and tosses (her) about, As one forgetting that (she) was his mother." The quarto presents the Queen emphatically denying that she knew of her husband's murder. In the second edition—published in the year of Oxford's death—the poet leaves her share in the crime to Heaven, under a mist; only God knows the extent of her guilt. So Shakespeare retained his bitterness toward his mother to the end.

Hamlet expostulates to his mother from an imaginary altitude of virtue, oblivious of the blemishes in his own character he had mentioned to Ophelia—his "too too sullied flesh"—and pours out his abhorrence for Gertrude's perfectly natural and now legitimate desire for wifely intimacy. Listening to the Prince preach, she feels ashamed of her passion, seeing in her soul "black and grained spots." She thrills her eloquent young man by comparing his words to knives. He condescends ironically to ask forgiveness for his virtue and departs proclaiming himself unhappily doomed to be Heaven's "scourge and minister."

In the first quarto a humbler Hamlet appeals to her Majesty:

> And mother, but assist me in revenge,
> And in his death your infamy shall die.

The grateful Gertrude responds to these words:

> Hamlet, I vow, by that Majesty
> That knows our thoughts, and looks into our hearts,
> I will conceal, consent, and do my best,
> What stratagem soe'er thou shalt devise.

It is possible that the treatment of the Prince's mother in the quarto of 1603 is the work of the stage-craftsman who arranged Shakespeare's text for the public that, "for the most part, are fit for nothing but inexplicable dumb-shows and noise." The artisan (Anthony Munday?) may have found the Gertrude of his master too perplexing a personality for the ordinary understanding and altered her along more popular maternal lines.

The Prince of Denmark in the larger version of the tragedy will make no compact with woman. Having vented his fury on her Majesty for preferring a "king of shreds and patches" to

"The expectancy and rose of fair state," he becomes charitable and willing to think well of her. After all, Claudius is mainly to blame for his mother's "stain." Shakespeare makes the villain declare, "The queen his mother Lives almost by his looks." But we do not hear her commending "a mother's care" to her son, like the Queen in the first quarto, who bids her Hamlet "Be wary of his presence, lest that he fail in that he goes about." That Gertrude showers a "thousand mother's blessings on my son." The Gertrude of Shakespeare's swordsmanship. But a moment later, when she dies crying, "O my dear Hamlet!...I am poison'd," he does not spring to sustain or avenge her. He turns his weapon on the king only when he discovers that he himself has been treacherously bled. Then he commands the assassin, "Follow my mother"—Where else but to hell? Thus the dramatist punished his own mother for abandoning him when he was twelve to become Charles Tyrell's bride.

The Ghost refers to some "foul crimes done in my days of nature." I have already mentioned the solitary crime recorded in the career of Sussex, inspired by his wish to end an Ireland war. The poet could not have been thinking of this gesture of over-zealous patriotism when he mentioned the crimes of Hamlet's father. He had in mind John de Vere, the sixteenth Earl of Oxford, who did commit a number of unknown crimes, for which the Duke of Somerset in 1548 frightened him into renouncing almost all his wealth.[83] Let us not forget that Hamlet singles out for description no feature of his father but his look of lordly threat. Our author's memory of that terrible eye surely concealed a childhood wish to extinguish it. Wherever we find father-worship we generally discover the child's yearning to uplift the father beyond humanity, a yearning that simultaneously gratifies the unconscious desire to do away with him and the conscious desire to gain salvation from such malignant thoughts by revering the planter of one's own seed. The blood of the father shed in the id redeems the ego of the son. And out of this "sacrifice" and redemption comes a new self-esteem, even the feeling of holiness. The tears of Hamlet on contemplating the metamorphosis of his father from flesh to spirituality are tears of relief as well as remorse. His relief manifests itself in laughter, in calling the majestic fantom "true-penny," after the coin that constantly turns up in exchange, and so on.

Meanwhile his malignant thoughts seek transference to objects which he considers deserving of hate. He encounters these easily enough in the real world (Claudius and Polonius) and in the world of art. Look at his weeping over the First Player's speech, which he requests on the spur of the moment—like a French falconer, flying at anything he sees. The Player had once declaimed this speech to Hamlet, apparently in private: "It was never acted; or, if it was, not above once; for the play, I remember, pleased not the million; 'twas caviar to the general." No marvel: its rhetoric sounds like the diligence of a juvenile English Seneca. "One speech in it," Hamlet confesses, "I chiefly loved; 'twas Eneas' tale to Dido; and thereabout of it especially where he speaks of Priam's slaughter." He follows with rapt attention the recital of the one way prince Pyrrhus butchered the father of Troy. His tears drop when the Player comes to the lines on Queen Hecuba's anguish at the sight of her mangled husband. The same mind that dwells with woe on the spectacle of father Priam's slaughter lingers with fond amusement on the vision of Polonius being butchered like a calf in the role of the murdered Caesar.

At this point in my analysis I will rest and reflect on the chance that the lost play quoted by Hamlet could have been a tragedy concerning Queen Dido of Carthage, perhaps composed by Oxford's friend Thomas Watson, after they had seen and heard William Gager's Latin play *Dido* enacted at Oxford University on June 11, 1583, under the supervision of the gifted mountebank George Peele.[84]

Obsession with patricide reveals itself even in the casual allusion that Polonius makes on the great Roman actor Roscius.

For the dramatist knew that the actor was once put on trial for this crime.

In a sense Polonius is right when he tells the King his notion of the cause of Hamlet's mental disorder:

> Yet I do believe
> The origin and commencement of his grief
> Sprung from neglected love.

The outcome of the dramatist's own love-frustration is "the general atmosphere of lechery" which the philologian Francis A. March long ago (in 1875) deplored in the play.[84a] Both mother- and father-love were "neglected" in Hamlet's case. Having learnt in his childhood more of hate than of love from his parents, the pristine exemplars of behavior, he developed in consequence of his psychic starvation a habit of holding libido for his own interior solace, and could never in truth love anyone else. Charles Arundel was not entirely wrong when he asserted that De Vere, "Though he love no man living for his heart, yet of all he most detesteth those that are nearly knit by nature."[85] That is why the Prince can honestly say, "Man delights not me; no, nor woman neither."

Polonius is mistaken in claiming the loss of his Ophelia to be the source of the Prince's disease. Our hero's method of communication with her suffices to prove that no love was lost between them. He writes to her artificially and talks sarcastically or obscenely, with never a note of kindness. He takes a queer pleasure in imagining the virgin endowed with a power of parthenogenesis, giving birth to maggots and monsters. (Act II, Scene 2) In the scene of her crazy songs Shakespeare plainly implies that she cared more for her father than the Prince. One of Earl Edward's reasons for parting from his Countess Anne was "That his wife was most directed by her father and mother"—a charge which he translated into terms of incest, according to my interpretation of *Pericles,*

Prince of Tyre.[85a] Our dramatist failed to clarify Hamlet's intentions toward the girl. Her brother and father obviously believe that he aimed at nothing more than fornication. Laertes declares that the prince will marry none but a lady capable of augmenting the fortitude and "health of the whole state." (Act I, Scene 3) The bridal choice of Hamlet, Laertes takes for granted, will be determined by the nobility, "the main voice of Denmark"—"that body Whereof he is the head." So we are led to decide that Ophelia did not have the ghost of a chance to be the Prince's bride.Queen Gertrude, on the contrary, hopes that the girl's qualities will restore Hamlet to peace and decency, "his wonted way." Later we hear that the Queen expected Ophelia to become Hamlet's wife. (Act V, Scene 1) The first quarto does not contain this hope. In the legend of Amleth told by Saxo Grammaticus and Belleforest, the girl loved by the hero is commanded by the king to lure him into fornication—a contrivance to prove that Amleth is not so stupid as he acts. The prince manages to enjoy her without his adversaries being aware. Shakespeare, however, could not bring himself to present his hero in a deed of cheap deceit and sensuality. Hamlet's intentions had to be honorable. When he cries, "I loved Ophelia," we are expected to believe him, despite the contrary testimony of his mute and brutal rejection of her, after brooding on his father's apparition, and his outspoken contempt for Ophelia's desire to be the mother of his children. Sincerely he advises her to enter a nunnery. Compare the statement of the duchess in *The Murder of Gonzago* that, if she remarries, she ought to be made an anchorite.

In my opinion, these visions of parturition, celibacy, and so forth, tormented the dramatist in March 1584, when the Earl of Oxford secretly suffered from shame because of the pregnancy of his wife soon after his return to living with her. To free himself from the torments, he created Hamlet.

The source of Ophelia's insanity is the collision in her soul between attachment to her father and sexual longing for Hamlet, his murderer. "They say the owl was a baker's daughter," she remarks. In her creator's mind when he wrote these words was the medieval legend of the baker's girl whom the Madonna's Mate transformed into an owl because she refused to give bread in charity to the hungry Christ.[86] On viewing this legend in the light of Ophelia's self-betrayal, the thought obtrudes that Shakespeare doomed her to madness for having refused love to Lord Hamlet, his own "Son of Man." She may have yielded her body to his chilled importuning, but filled him with her terror of failure and sin. This seems to be the hidden significance of her song about the girl who surrendered her maiden-head on the eve of Saint Valentine's day to a young man who promised to marry her.

By Gis (Jesus) and by Saint Charity,
Attack, and fie for shame!
Young men will do't, if they come to't.
By Cock, they are to blame.

Shakespeare, in his phases of Platonic morality, always made a sharp distinction between such "country matters" and true love. In his estimation the true love of Ophelia went to no man but Polonius. Meditating on this attachment, he would certainly remember another legend concerning the owl, told by his favorite poet Ovid in the second book of his *Metamorphoses*. According to the Roman writer's account, the original owl was the girl Nyctimene who was changed to the bird in penalty for incest with her father.

Skulls well cultivated with the lore of Wales, listening to Ophelia tell the crowned heads of Denmark the origin of the owl in continental legend, would have been reminded of the grim myth of Huan ap Don, who was killed by his wife's lover Gronw with her horrible help. For this (according to *The White Goddess* by Robert Graves, 1948) the quean-accomplice was changed to an owl.

Ophelia sighs to Gertrude, "the beauteous majesty of Denmark," that "your true love" can be recognized by his costume of a pilgrim to the shrine of Saint Iago at Compostella in Spain. The same costume in which Romeo first made love to Juliet in her father's house. The two lovers of Verona met and married in summer. The maiden with whom Ophelia seems to identify herself lost her virginity on the eve of February 14. I cannot help hazarding the guess that the date held an amorous meaning for Anne Cecil and Edward de Vere. Parenthetically, let me mention here that the symbolism of the rosemary given by Ophelia can be found in A *Handful of Pleasant Delights*, a collection of poems published in 1584, the year to which I attribute the primary *Hamlet*. Several early-Victorian commentators on the madness of Ophelia have declared their conviction that her random allusions and melodies flowed "from once hushed resting-places far within her memory," going back to some ballads and bawdiness she had listened to in infancy.[87] Mrs Anna Brownell Jameson ventured the suggestion that a lass like Ophelia may have enjoyed the care of an "old nurse (who) sang her to sleep" with such lascivious lullabies in her babyhood. If they had likewise traced the fantasies of Hamlet to erotic stimulation in childhood, they would have saved psychoanalysis a good deal of work.

They could have connected the apparition in his mother's chamber with the shocking vision which Freud designates the primal scene, the revelation to the child of his parents' libidinal bond. The two quartos of *Hamlet* assert that the Ghost of the dead king confronts his son here "in his habit as he lived." Only the first quarto contains the stage direction, "Enter the Ghost in his night-gown." The sight so terrifies the Prince that he prays for angels' help. He hears a voice rebuking him for the "lapse in time and passion" between his first resolve to slay King Claudius, and the present conflict with his mother. The fantom asserts that his purpose is "almost blunted" by long brooding on his mother's lust instead of his father's death. The apparition looks on him piteously and he feels like weeping. Gertrude interrupts the delusion. Hamlet insists it was not a delusion, offering to repeat what had been spoken as if sheer (obsessional) repetition were proof of a lucid head. Free of the fantom, he compulsively returns to the theme of his mother's vice. He orders her not to go that night to his uncle's bed. In the quarto of 1603 he pleads: "O mother, if ever you did my dear father love..." The major version allows us to surmise that she never loved the elder Hamlet. Yet the reason the Prince hates her, and must fortify his heart against the wish to follow Nero's road to matricide, is precisely the love she had manifested for his father. He never could endure the thought of the royal bed of Denmark being "A couch for luxury." The late King's tenderness toward her, which young Hamlet recalls in his first soliloquy, must have kindled a generous emotion in the Queen. Her son remembers the signs of one:

> Heaven and earth!
> Must I remember? Why, she would hang on him,
> As if increase of appetite had grown
> By what it fed on.

The overtones of erotic feeling in the speech betray the jealousy of boyhood on watching her cling to his father. He probably endeavored to separate them, like so many children who see their parents kiss. His disgust—decrease of appetite—at the spectacle and his horror on imagining them both in bed were fiercely repressed and denied outlet until the second wedding of his mother provided a stage-worthy motive and cue for his indignation. The infantile rage became respectable; or so he thought. I have estimated the scope of the primal scene in the case of the child Edward de Vere more intensively in my essay "Early Errors," a study of his first comedy. (See the *International Journal of Psycho-Analysis*, April 1955).

Killing Polonius behind the arras, Hamlet demonstrates what he once wished to do to the man who originally "intruded" to rescue his Queen from the infantile violence of the Prince. The blood of the old Chamberlain gives him for the moment so much satisfaction that he forgets his obligation to kill the King. He counsels Gertrude to refrain from her husband's embrace for the next three nights; then she will gradually get accustomed to existing without it. What clearer testimony could one ask for to prove that Hamlet has no genuine intention to do away with Claudius?

It is noteworthy that Shakespeare made a Chamberlain of the father whom Hamlet murdered. Traditionally the post of Chamberlain belonged to the man assigned by majesty to guard the royal bedroom. When we remember that, for most of the years in which the Earl of Oxford played courtier to Elizabeth, her Chamberlain was Thomas Radcliff, Earl of Sussex, the idea inevitably springs up that De Vere may occasionally have considered the chance of his friend being murdered in order for a criminal to gain access to her Majesty's sleeping room. If Charles W. Barrell and I are right in regarding the title of Chamberlain in Shakespeare's theatrical company as an ambiguity masking the function of Oxford, the Lord Great Chamberlain of England, in the place of the Queen's Chamberlain, then we have here another mode by which the young Earl usurped in fantasy the room of a father-surrogate. I suppose he unconsciously resented the superiority of Sussex, and did not realize that in slaying the Chamberlain Polonius he killed in effigy the Earl his benefactor, merged with the image of William Cecil. It now occurs to me that in stabbing the Chamberlain, Hamlet cries out, "A rat!" And the first syllable of Radcliff's name was frequently written "Rat." A cliff-rat might easily be confused with a mole, the animal emblematic of Hamlet's Ghost.

D

If there is any episode in the tragedy of the Dane where we may expect to unveil the real driving force behind his actions, it is the play within the play. (I regret that I was unable, before venturing on this analysis and since, to peruse Otto Rank's article, "Das 'Schauspiel' in Hamlet," in *Imago*, IV (1915) 41-51.) We encounter in the world of sleep a parallel phenomenon, the dream within a dream, from the principles of which we can deduce the meaning of Hamlet's little play. What motivates the dream within a dream appears to be a longing to deny the reality of the wish or instinctual gratification which constitutes the goal of the complete dream. It ostentatiously creates the illusion that the craving it fulfills is simply an illusion, make-believe, and this trick prevents exposure of the drive inspiring the dream proper. Unmasking the drive would produce anxiety and wake the author up. In a similar manner the dramatist is moved to stage the play within a play. By this device he hopes to show that the desire which struggles for outright utterance in the main work has no more substance than a show of "false fire." It does not matter, the author seems to protest; there is no offense meant—I am innocent of the wickedness which the whole play appears to disclose. *The Murder of Gonzago* was thus designed to testify that Hamlet at least had a "free soul"; it touches him not with terror. His writer employs the device to demonstrate the protagonist's virtue: behold, our hero, far from being himself guilty of incestuous greed and patricidal lust, comes forward courageously to unmask and brand the man who has actually done these things. The little drama will catch the conscience of King Claudius. If it fails to expose the criminal to the world, says the Prince, then

> my imaginations are as foul
> As Vulcan's stithy.

(Vulcan, you recall, was the crippled god who forged a snare in which to catch his wife Venus and Mars making love.) Unfortunately for the amateur stage-manager, his poorly constructed trap works only well enough to convince one man, his philosophic friend Horatio. The King's occulted guilt is not provoked to "unkennel in one speech." His conscience receives ample warning of the plot with the dumb-show that comes before the verse of which our "jig-maker" is so proud.

Artistically "The Mouse Trap" is indeed a wretched piece of work. The married pair in it are titled King and Queen; but Hamlet calls the former a duke; almost immediately after, he restores the royal title, indicating Lucianus is "nephew to the king." In the first quarto Gonzago and his wife are titled Duke and Duchess. We are puzzled by the name Hamlet gives his play. "The Rat Trap" would have been more appropriate, as when the Prince cries out "A rat" in trapping the King's agent behind the arras. The only character called "mouse" in the drama is the Queen. (Act III, Scene 4) Could Hamlet have really intended his play to catch the conscience of the Queen? He seems to have looked forward to a scene in which "the murderer gets the love of Gonzago's wife"—an exhibition of female perversity like the scene in Shakespeare's *Richard III* where the protagonist conquers the heart of Lady Anne, whom he had cruelly widowed. Gertrude, however, is never convicted of any law violation. The Ghost damns her as an adulteress, Hamlet believes her "stained": yet he dares not accuse her openly. When Claudius makes his first admission of guilt to himself, in the Third Act, he speaks of "my deed," meaning the fratricide. Adultery is not on his conscience. Not once does he think of it in the soliloquy on his sins. The first quarto, in an effort to be more consistent, has Claudius confess in solitude "the adulterous fault I have committed." Hamlet does not charge him with it in the end of the play. The Prince's own play is mostly concerned with the implicit charge that the

Queen was a hypocrite when she vowed love and devotion to her first throne-mate.

The little drama that Hamlet selected to snare his stepfather's conscience is not a story of fratricide, tho the Prince, profoundly acquainted as he was with theatrical lore, could have easily found one for his purpose. The classic legend of Merope, for example: here the king Kresphontes is murdered by his brother and the usurper of his kingdom weds the widow, then is killed by the late king's son. A subject recommended by Aristotle, and popular in Italy in Oxford's time. Instead of a tale of brother-murder, Hamlet chooses one in which a nephew kills his uncle. Lucianus does what Hamlet only dreams. The nephew in Hamlet's piece poisons the king or duke for his "estate" and to win the love of his wife. Hamlet eventually poisons his King, for three reasons: Claudius had deprived him of a monopoly of his mother's love, and obtained the crown by the acclaim of Denmark's "better wisdoms."—

> Popp'd in between the election and my hopes—

and conspired to kill him. Claudius, it is true, does not plot against his nephew's life until he has evidence of Hamlet's homicidal impulse toward him.

The young man's casual reference to his hopes of getting the crown after his father's death casts a weird light on his posture of unselfishness. He regards himself as Heaven's minister, born to set right the "time," meaning the state, which he judges "out of joint." His two friends Rosenkrantz and Guildenstern, who have been acquainted with him since early youth, say that he suffers from ambition. Denmark, they tell him, "is too narrow for your mind." He protests that he could be restricted to a very small area and still "count myself a king of infinite space, were it not that I have bad dreams." Mysterious dreams prevent him from enjoying obscurity when he sang, "My mind to me a kingdom is." Guildenstern insists that the Prince's bad dreams have their roots in ambition. Knowing that this was the unpardonable sin for which Lucifer turned into the Devil, for which Shakespeare's Brutus kills his Caesar, and his Macbeth wades in blood, we do not wonder that Hamlet repudiates the accusation of the two courtiers. Yet when he meditates on Fortinbras, another prince with a father slain, seeking an empire for himself, Hamlet lauds him for having a "spirit with divine ambition puffed." Later he remarks about Laertes, who has led a rabble to storm the royal castle—a mob demanding not justice for his father's tenebrous death, but the crown for their young leader—

> By the image of my cause I see
> The portraiture of his.

In other words, Laertes had a just cause for revolt in his suspicion that Polonius fell a victim to foul play. The rabble clamors for Laertes to be king and he says nothing to indicate that he would not take the throne; he does not rebuke his followers for rioting in order to put a mere student, a college hotspur, on the throne. By the image of this presumption we can see the conscious goal Hamlet had set himself. Did he deserve to govern Denmark? His creator apparently thought, yes. He puts on the lips of Prince Fortinbras, who knows scarcely anything about Hamlet, the last word of appraisal:

> For he was likely, had he been put on,
> To have prov'd most royal.

Despite Shakespeare's toil to justify this belief and the mazy ways of his hero to man, I think the ultimate verdict will go against him. He protests too much that the Prince is on the side of the angels. Not only does he portray his dear Dane as a mirror of all the splendid qualities advocated in *The Courtier* by Baldassare Castiglione (Act IV, Scene 7), as one

"Most generous and free from all contriving"—shortly after his Majesty had detected Hamlet setting theatrical traps for him. Up to the utterance of this tribute, Claudius has constantly eyed his nephew as a man brooding over some grudge, bound to hatch danger. The Prince himself admits he has "something dangerous" in him. He denies, however, that he acts rashly, on impulse of mere spleen. Then did he deliberately insult Laertes at the grave of his sister? NO: "I am very sorry, good Horatio, That Laertes I forgot myself"—

> But sure the bravery of his grief did put me
> Into a towering passion.

He could not let the miserable orphan grieve in his own fashion in peace. He felt somehow challenged, histrionically. "Nay, an thou'lt mouth, I'll rant as well as thou." In the presence of Osric he is prompted to a like discourtesy: he cannot resist the temptation to mouth-mimicry. After losing control of his passion for showing off, by the dead body of Ophelia, he speaks as if ignorant of the reason for her brother's anger: "What is the reason that you use me thus? I lov'd you ever," he adds, as if whatever gestures of fraternal affection he had once displayed now excused him from the consequences of his effrontery. "I lov'd you ever,—but it is no matter," he sighs, with the same wit that Sir Walter Ralegh dreaded in the Earl of Oxford,"...dog will have his day." Afterward he tells the son of Polonius that he did not purpose evil in killing the man who hid behind his mother's curtain. He compares it to an accidental arrow shot, which "hurt my brother." He appeals to Laertes' generosity with the argument that he wronged him under the goad of madness. We need not spend any space discussing Hamlet's frost-blooded cruelty to Rosencrantz and Guildenstern, his forging a letter of state to have them executed in England for no other reason than that they have pryed into his strange conduct, in obedience to the King, and chided him for ambition. Behavior like this moved the critic George Steevens to write severely about the "immoral tendency" of Hamlet's character. "It is obvious to the most careless spectator or reader," Steevens declares, "that he kills the King at last to revenge himself, and not his father." The Prince turns his sword on the criminal King only when his own skin is assailed.

The truth is that Hamlet is radically immature and sick. The root of his sickness lies in the core of his soul. "Thou woulds't not think," he confides to Horatio, "how ill all's here about my heart." Mark Akenside, the physician and poet, told Steevens "the conduct of Hamlet was every way unnatural and indefensible, unless he were to be regarded as a young man whose intellects were in some degree impaired by his own misfortunes."[88] I beg to differ from Dr Akenside and the psychiatrists who endorse his opinion. The misfortunes that happened to Hamlet cannot account for his fondness of self-display, his sense of superiority to custom and law. Salvador de Madariaga correctly points to egotism as the Prince's main trouble and the fountainhead of his tragedy. My own diagnosis of Hamlet's malady would place it in the category of hysteria, bordering on narcissic derangement or paranoia. (In a conversation with Dr Theodor Reik [December 2, 1955], he informed me that he had concluded Hamlet's disease is paranoid. For a preliminary statement of this view of Shakespeare's sickness, see "Othello's Obsessions," *American Imago* [June 1952]).

We are under no obligation to take Hamlet's word for the prophetic powers of his soul. If we approached the court of Elsinore as strangers to Shakespeare and heard the Prince condemn his mother's second marriage as bad and fated to end badly, we might regard him as morbidly suspicious. Suppose one lends credence to the soldiers who think they have seen their soldier-king patrolling his castle as a ghost on the nights of a national emergency. Why should one lend any credence to the solitary youth who claims to have received a personal message from the ghost—a message bearing no relation to the crisis or war? The pathological nature of his vanity and distrust is revealed when he murmurs, on learning about the soldiers' vision, "I doubt some foul play." He suspected his uncle before his interview with the Ghost, and so hears exactly what he wished to believe.

Yet the first person he turns against, in the ecstasy of the cause which has lifted him out of depression, is the filial weakling Ophelia, who nearly worships him. Next we see him mocking the Lord Chamberlain, her father, who helped elect his uncle King but did Hamlet no other "harm." Meeting the two men to whom, according to his mother, he adhered more than any others living, he acts wary at once. His feeling of persecution shows itself: "I am most dreadfully attended." With the exception of Horatio, a soldier or two, and the players, he views everyone around him as an antagonist. And these friendly inferiors he usually treats like a remote critic of mortality. We have already observed the delusions of grandeur which he nourishes along with his revulsion from society. It would be tedious to review further the symptoms of the Prince; there are more than enough to illustrate any text on the paranoid personality. A student might well compare them with the clinical picture of narcissic neurosis in the case of the judge Daniel Schreber analyzed by Freud.[89] The Dane's disease lacks the systematic and blatantly logical character of paranoia. Salvation from his sickness luckily uplifted the poet from a number of vital springs. His vanity was dampened and reduced under the discipline of his humility as a working man of the vulgate and theater, the modesty of art. The immense pleasure he derived from laughter, especially at the expense of his own stupidities, saved him from the extreme penalty of autoapotheosis. Deeper than these benefits of his genius and culture ran his gift of imitating the grimaces and mouthings of people, to whom he transferred the energy of his neurosis and so formed fruitful social ties, when they patiently received his "medicine." Together with this impulse to show people with his face how they looked and spoke, he retained all his days the strong urge to show his whole self off, delightful and divine as on the day he first dawned. And this preserved him also from the isolation of insanity, steering him permanently toward communication with his kind, making himself clear.

One feature of Hamlet's malady or health invites our particular scrutiny, his religion. His "antic disposition" seldom interferes with his piety. He counsels Horatio and Marcellus to go "as your business and desire shall point you—For every man hath business and desire;" as for his own "poor part," he will go pray. He adores prayer. He believes that the paramount scoundrel in Denmark will ascend to Heaven instantly if he is killed while praying. Yet the theologians have found it a bewildering job to determine the framework of Hamlet's religion. A kind of Christianity, of course. One exclusively Shakespeare's own, while closer to the Catholic than the Protestant. Its faith and charity permit a purgatory for criminals as well as return from the "undiscovered country" beyond the tomb. One of its divine canons prohibits suicide altho the God of Christendom had never done so explicitly. Hamlet, however, apprehends the will of his God almost perfectly, as if he were one of those "secretaries of the Holy Ghost" who, John Donne said, wrote the Old and New Testaments. Hamlet's Lord countenanced his slaying of Polonius, Rosencrantz, Guildenstern, and Claudius. In shedding their blood he served as a true liege and minister of his Lord. We have already noticed how Shakespeare identified his hero with Jesus Christ in the legend of the baker's daughter who became an owl. By the logic of these epiphanies we are led to the conclusion that the Lord of the dramatist must have verily worn the semblance of Hamlet himself.

From the outset Hamlet conceives himself as a born savior. The poet's faith in his supernatural mission is unconsciously clarified by the lines of Horatio and Marcellus after the latter has voiced his opinion about the rottenness in the state. Horatio assures him, "Heaven will direct it." "Nay," replies Marcellus, "let's follow him," meaning the Lord Hamlet. A Christian cult with these facets must have struck the contemporaries of Shakespeare with wonder. In the light of it (or should we say the darkness?) we can understand why Lord Henry Howard and Francis Southwell could accuse the Earl of Oxford of deriding the Bible and preaching atheism, while Andrew Trollop, who served the Earl for eleven years as a deputy steward—"during all that time being privy not only of his public dealings, but also of his private doings and secret intents—found and knew him indued with special piety..." Trollop's testimony calls to mind the confirmation by Thomas Kyd of his unknown Lord's religion. Kyd reported that his master could never endure the sight or name of Christopher Marlowe after he heard of Marlowe's avowals of atheism. "The form of divine prayer used daily in his Lordship's house," Kyd wrote, kept reprobates like Christopher at a distance.[90] A look at the noble Ashbourne portrait of Shakespeare, now known to be a portrait of Edward de Vere (painted by Cornelis Ketel about 1580) instructs us about the image in which our dramatist fashioned his God.

Now identification with deity in the carnal imagery of the unconscious translates into unity with parentage. To the extent that we can ascertain its working, we find the unconscious favors one mode of identifying with the father and mother, a process of ingestion which has been correctly compared to cannibalism. The infant mind consumes the parental body in imagination. It incorporates the latter's flesh for pleasure, with elemental love; without love it could not enjoy the idea of mingling the sweet mother and strong father with its own flesh and blood. That child of the species, the savage, turns cannibal for the same reason, wishing to hold in his entrails the admirable qualities of the individual he eats. Envy and hate go along with savage love. There must be enough hate to destroy the object desired, even in fantasy. Once possessed by the child within, the archaic psyche, the parent turns into an idol incarnating the aspirations and power-propulsions of the self. If the mother lives in comparative harmony with the father, this idol takes on dynamic feminine aspects and develops into an oracle of family authority, the superego, without specific character or sex, and comes in consequence to represent society. Under circumstances of conflict between mother and father, the impersonal superego turns monster and attacks society or the self. Fluctuating between unity with the ego and alienation from it, the superego concentrates into its clutch the aggressive energy at the disposal of the mind, and manifests itself as conscience and moral taskmaster, a despot more or less enlightened but always enjoying its savagery. Before the ego can exert full control over the motor resources of its organism, it must arrive at peace and concord with that monitor. The pursuit of happiness aims at nothing else. One of the means of attaining this harmony is humor, the mood in which our poet, talking thru the mask of the little demon Puck, exclaimed: "Lord, what fools these mortals be!" The criminal mind has other means, preferably perverse, of achieving the syntonic mood with its father-in-fantasy. Paraphrenia varies these techniques and invents its own.

According to the trailblazing psychoanalytic doctrine on the genesis of paranoia, the malady had its germ in homoerotic attraction toward the individual believed to be persecuting the sufferer or exciting his jealousy. In defense of the ego fighting waves of impulses of lust for one of the same sex, the victim systematically erects offensive devices, projecting his desires and the outrage and hostility they induce to the object of his unconscious love. To protect himself from the sea of woes inside his soul, he takes up arms against the apparitions of his own sex who seem to threaten him with drowning in that sea. He discovers his own psychic menaces in the body frames of those who suggest his alluring ghosts. Freud made this diagnosis of paranoia from a literary case-history, the autobiography of Daniel Schreber, a German jurist who had succeeded in working his way back to sanity to an amazing extent, clinging to his main delusions. Dr Ida Macalpine and her son Richard Hunter made a more thoro survey of the Schreber case, comparing it with clinical records of their own experience, and reached the conclusion that Freud had made a grave mistake. What the paranoiac suffered from, in their judgment, was not repressed homosexuality, but a frightening bewilderment, inability to determine his or her actual sex.[91]

Before I became acquainted with the Macalpine-Hunter diagnosis, my analysis of Hamlet had led me to a like conclusion about his case.

The histrionic Prince of Denmark, insofar as he indulges in politics and philosophy, I decided (over twenty years ago) wavers on the brink of paranoia. He vacillates between the whirlpool of hysteria and the rock of melancholy which he is tempted to regard as a haven for his brain. His mother pictures the process in her comment on his raving at Ophelia's burial ground:

> This is mere madness:
> And thus a while the fit will work on him;
> Anon, as patient as the female dove,
> When that her golden couplets are disclos'd,
> His silence will sit drooping.

It is in this female mood of his melancholy that Hamlet nurtures unaware certain dreams of homosexual longing for the King, inspired by despair of winning a woman's lasting love. He cannot honor Ophelia's love because of his conviction that she is disloyal to him for her father's sake.

Where is the proof that the Prince is attracted unaware, by his animal magnetism toward King Claudius? When I asked myself that question, I remembered Hamlet's protestations of deadly enmity to the King and paraphrased the wise comment of Ophelia on the Duchess Baptista Gonzago: The Prince protests too much. He seems to be storming in order to quell an eloquence inside that points out the King's attractive traits. Claudius had charming qualities, we know by the witnesses of his election to the monarchy and Gertrude's affection for him. The Ghost acknowledges a kind of "witchcraft" in the wit of his Majesty. Moreover Hamlet himself bears witness to the graces of Claudius. He inscribes in his tablet of memorable observations that "a man may smile and smile, and be a villain," as if he needed this trivial record to shake off the spell of his uncle's curled lips. The Prince pretends to be astonisht that a "vice of kings" like Gertrude's lover could be so adored on coming to the throne that people paid fantastic prices for his portrait in miniature. With metaphysical humor Hamlet remarks, "There is something in this more than natural, if philosophy could find it out." But Hamlet not only believes in witchcraft (persuaded by fidelity to the idea of his own thought partaking in almightiness); he believes in divine providence and a celestial shaping of human ends, precisely like Arthur Golding, the Calvinist brother of Countess Margaret de Vere. So the advancement of his rival did indeed strike the poet as supernatural. The King then is a minister of Heaven like Hamlet himself. The Prince sums up his sentiments about Claudius in his very first words in the play: "A little more than kin, and less than kind." His feeling for the King's consanguinity is so intense that he can only subdue it by ridicule. He refers to Claudius and Gertrude as "My uncle-father and aunt-mother," and later argues to his stepfather that he is correct in calling his Majesty "dear mother," because—"father and mother is man and wife, man and wife is one flesh, and so, my mother." His feeling of kinship with Claudius is accompanied by the sullen insistence that his uncle is unkind to him. We are given no cause for Hamlet's thinking so. The King is always considerate, patient and easy-going with his capricious nephew.

The fact is that the two men have more in common than agnate blood and their identity of goals. The essential sympathy between their personalities emerges in mysterious likeness in the significance of their names. "Claudius" comes from a Latin stem meaning crippled, lame. And "Hamlet" derives from an Anglo-Saxon verb hamelod which means mutilated, hamstrung.[92] (Compare the hero's evocation of limping Vulcan in his simile for the ugliness of his imagination.) In Freudian terms, both his Majesty and Hamlet are victims of a complex of inferiority having its root in the boyhood dread of castration. Their unconscious grievance and identical ambitions make Hamlet and Claudius kinsmen more than plain consanguinity could. Yet Hamlet revolts against their emotional proximity. His ego-ideal of virility will not allow it.

The King's name, you know, is never pronounced in dialog. Shakespeare's choice of the word Claudius for the royal scoundrel is peculiar since it is a name that he gave (in Italian form) to the romantic heroes in *Much Ado About Nothing* and *Measure for Measure*, two characters who clearly portray the poet's own youth. We can tell the name haunted him by the fact that he called one of his courtiers of Denmark "Claudio." We never meet this gentleman, whose position in the plot casually links him as a go-between to Hamlet and his Majesty. He is a fantom, silently suggesting that the poet felt bound to station close to Claudius a figure of himself disguised like one of his two Italian lovers.

The uncle's success in politics and love impresses the nephew with an unbearable sense of his own faultful virility. Hamlet's beard and his "continual practice" in warlike sports only deepen his feeling of depleted manhood. He betrays it by showing anxiety wherever he suspects anyone of hinting that his masculinity is not what it should be. Thus, in fencing with Laertes, he calls for his opponent's "best violence." "I am afeard," says Hamlet, "you make a wanton of me." Alone or with his intimate Horatio, the hero is less reluctant to confess his womanly traits. He deplores the way he shrewishly vents his emotions, comparing himself to a whore. Near the end of the tragedy he confides to Horatio that his heart is afflicted with "a kind of gain-giving as would perhaps trouble a woman." It was Frank Harris, I believe, who first acknowledged how Shakespeare startled him by the streaks of femininity revealed whenever the critic probed below the surface of the poet's protagonists. Samuel Butler, the prodigal biologian, seems to have been the first to perceive and publish the androgyne tide in our dramatist's blood. But he went no farther than Shakespeare's *Sonnets Reconsidered* (London 1899).

E

Hamlet's femininity shows itself in ways more subtle than hysterical outpouring of words or flutterings of the heart. His passion for exhibiting himself may be said to spring from the female in his soul. When he pictures himself applying for membership in a troop of actors, he envisages a youth with two French damask roses on his shoes and a veritable "forest of feathers." This plumage reminds me of the picture that Barnabe Rich drew, in his *Farewell to Military Profession* (1581), of a London gentleman extremely attracted to French fashions in dress. Rich's description, says the biographer of Edward de Vere, "makes it practically certain that he is caricaturing Lord Oxford." The gentleman was encountered in the Strand going toward Westminster—near the home of William Cecil. He rode "a footcloth nag, apparelled in a French ruff, a French cloak, a French hose, and in his hand a great fan of feathers, bearing them up (very womanly) against the side of his face." Rich remarks he thought it "impossible that there might a man be found so foolish as to make himself a scorn to the world to wear so womanish a toy; but rather thought it had been some shameless woman that had disguised herself like a man in our hose and our cloaks." The gentleman's beard did not lessen his observer's scorn. "I saw three following that were his men," says Rich, "and taking the hindermost by the arm I asked him what gentlewoman his master was. But the fellow, not understanding my meaning, told me his master's name and so departed." Rich went on reflecting about the possible use of that fan of feathers, in vain.[93] He could afford to make fun of Oxford's daring in apparel; the Earl was in disgrace and an exile from the Court. Furthermore the satirist had the powerful Sir Christopher Hatton to protect him. Whatever the function of Oxford's forest of feathers, there can be no denying that he strove with all his fortune to set the pattern of costume for his country. His expense accounts tell us in part of his sartorial aspiration and caprice. From the time of his adventures in Italy and France, and the return to England with his innovation of perfumed gloves, he tried ardently to become for his country "The glass of fashion and the mold of form." Evidently it did not occur to him that one purpose of all this display might be the allurement of handsome men. When it finally did disquiet him he seems to have solaced his conscience with the reflection that it was merely one of those habits "that too much overleaven the form of plausive manners."

In De Vere's experiments with homosexuality—on which we have only the testimony of his enemies—he probably confined himself to play the dominant male. They accused him of buggery, of maltreating various boys. "Auratio the Italian boy complained how horribly my Lord had abused him and yet would not give him anything." Once the Earl confided to his Catholic friend William Cornwallis that he wished to have a priest to whom he could confess his "ill life that way with so many boys..."[94] In the company of these pretty and immature admirers the poet could play the dictator and lordly lover without experiencing the challenge to virility and menace of genital loss which he endured in his intercourse with girls. Still he must have suffered shame in yielding to this sort of love. It conflicted with his earliest principles of manliness, his vision of the true courtier, soldier and scholar. He strove to conquer his desire for it and out of his strife extruded his neurotic eccentricity.

The memory of the Italian lad whom Oxford selected for one of his trials in pederasty may have given our dramatist the name of Hamlet's singular friend. The name of another dear friend of the Prince brings to my mind the memory of a daring soldier whom Oxford once loved and lost. I am thinking of the jester Yorick and the military adventurer Rowland York. Chateaubriand noticed that Hamlet speaks of Yorick as of a woman.[95] It would be more correct to say that he talks about the buffoon in language more appropriate to a partner in sodomy: "he hath born me on his back a thousand times…those lips that I have kissed I know not how oft." The story of Oxford's affair with York has been told, or rather pieced together in my analysis of *Othello*, the tragedy in which De Vere betrayed the allurement and revulsion he felt in the presence of Sir Philip Sidney. In *Hamlet* he betrayed the same emotions toward Sidney's uncle, Robert Dudley, the man whom he deemed the most diabolic of Protestants.

Shakespeare enacted the masquerade of imperial maleness to fortify his ego against unconscious desire to submit his body to ravishment by a man. He recoiled violently from a wish to reverse the roles. In the presence of strong magnetic men he felt his reason whelmed by erotic emotion which, rising into consciousness, summoned him to fawn on masculine strength. To repel the covert lust he exhausted the weapons of his ego. He spurned and laughed at sycophants. He imitated the part of the conquerors whom he profoundly wished would vanquish him. Between revels in delusions of supremacy he nursed the suspicion that the men he unconsciously adored had evil designs on him. If they vexed him he fell into ecstasies of persecution; if they crossed his will he absorbed his soul, adorning his frame, fretting tenderly over his sanctity. "Let the candied tongue lick absurd pomp." He would not render to Caesar the tribute he thought Caesar most coveted. And of course he went in quest of desirable women, and found them above all in beauties with vigorous masculine currents like Bess Tudor and Anne Vavasor.

In his revulsion from the homoerotic desire his ego underwent a backward drive to what promised to be safer modes of sexuality. This internal flight carried him from the peril of the narcissic quest of love-objects bearing a resemblance to his dark ideal of virility or his own good looks in puberty to the narcissic satisfaction that needed nobody to love. Autoerotic occupations were the ghastly remembrance of this—in reality his longing for wounds and moles and ailments, and studying the changes of age in his skin. Of course his vanity found no haven in the infantile felicities of the anal zone. Not only because it reminded him of sodomy. His fastidious sensuality abhorred filth except in the rarefied form of wit. In the person of Duke Orsino in *Twelfth Night* he proudly announced that his nobility did not prize any quantity of "dirty lands." He repeated the announcement in *Hamlet*, voicing disdain for rent-wringers, "spacious in dirt." He felt defiled by the retention of real estate just as he shrank from the slime his imagination discerned in money. His mental regression went beyond the sphere bordering on the genital to a resting-place in the phase of oral erotics, where pampering his palate became nearly obsessional. Under the impulsion of the libido of his mouth he grew fat, like Hamlet, and scant of breath. He, "the mold of form"!

We have noticed how Hamlet associates love with "increase of appetite." He translates his mother's affection for her second husband into the metaphor of leaving the food of a fair mountain to batten on a moor. The ancient notion that the sun engenders life in corpses brings to his mind's eye the picture of a god kissing carrion. When he feels at last capable of attacking the King, his eagerness expresses itself in buccal lust: "now could I drink hot blood." Revenge he visualizes in the act of fattening birds of prey with the offal of his uncle's meat.

He even thinks of his father's sepulcher in mouth-imagery, giving the grave jaws. The prince's oral libido has been so richly cultivated that he, an amateur poet, can instruct veteran actors in the act of dramatic speech. In fact for him a drama is not so much deeds as words. Several investigators of his language have pointed out Hamlet's preference for metaphors of lip and tongue. A flattering courtier strikes him as a candied tongue licking pomp. A lackey of the King is like an apple in an ape's jaw. The frustration of his royal hopes recalls the proverbial starving horse. His father's burden of sin calls up to his interior eye a vision of the old man "full of bread." Asked how he "fares" or gets along, he responds as if the King had asked how he fed: "I eat the air, promise-crammed. You cannot feed capons so." He extols the man of even temper and judgment as one whose heart is not a pipe for fortune to blow at random. Bitterly he likens his own spirit to such an instrument: "Sblood, do you think I am easier to be played on than a pipe?" Hamlet's favorite oath seems to be "God's blood." (In the course of Charles Arundel's indictment of the Earl of Oxford there is a note revealing the early and enduring interest of De Vere in the sensation of blood on his palate: "I speak not," Arundel wrote, "of his tasting blood in infancy, which almost prefigured a damnation."[96])

Hamlet dwells with relish on a fancy of Polonius being devoured by "a convocation of politic worms"—doubtless recalling the Diet of Worms convoked by the Emperor Charles V in 1521: "Your worm," says the Prince, "is your only emperor for diet." When Shakespeare wrote that sentence he was well aware that the French word for worm is ver. In the cemetery scene the imperial creature turns up as "My Lady Worm." Male or female, De Vere, I feel certain, was titillated by an obscure sense of kinship with the tiny eater of the dead. The poet's curiosity in trials of the palate induced him to the boast implicit in Hamlet's question to Laertes, whether he would dare to compete with him in swallowing easel (vinegar) or chewing crocodile meat. With almost all these utterances of oral-erotic fascination there runs a current of truculent feeling that mounts to sadism. This cruelty in Hamlet's regressive libido gets a mordant articulation in his joke about Osric's display of courtesy. He pictures the gentleman as a baby behaving elegantly even at his mother's breast: "A did comply, sir, with his dug before 'a sucked it." Note the possessive pronoun. One imagines that the infant Hamlet was less delicate, perhaps dictatorial, with Gertrude's teat.

Here, in the fastidious ferocity of Hamlet's mouth-oriented nervous extravagance, would I locate the heart of his mystery. This is the "vicious mole" of his character, and unconsciously his creator knew it all the time, for the word mole was the mot juste to a cosmopolitan mind acquainted with the German maul, meaning mouth, and capable of the Germanic pun of Hamlet on kin and kind.

Shakespeare could not rest content with libidinous eating and drinking or any other oral activity, for his demonic soul was bound to associate the pleasure with pederastic osculation. From the ghastly remembrance of this—in reality his longing for passivity in perversion—he found very few refuges. His favorite, I suppose, was the temporary exultation of his masculine self in the act of masturbation. More urethral than genital, his maleness could delight in its reveries and day-delusions only for brief intervals. Then he would chastise himself for childishness, for lowering his virility to such a mixture of discretion and cowardice. With laughing bravado he could call the hero of its fantasies "Will Shakespeare." Will in Elizabethan English signified sex-drive. Later he would mock its pretense of potency with the funny name Jack Falstaff, for a caricature of his soul. Disgust with boyish retreats from the contests of men and women would verily afflict his organs of taste. Out of this mood he would climb with facile celerity by spitting venom, sarcasm, paranoid hate.

He fancied that Leycester, the merry politician, whose handsome exterior was alleged to hide a conscience loaded with innumerable crimes, would be glad to seek his destruction. Dudley consented to the destruction of Oxford's beloved cousin Thomas Howard the Duke of Norfolk. He plotted for the downfall of Norfolk's brother-in-law, the Earl of Sussex, and the bruit ran with bibulous liberty that he had made a cuckold of the noblest of English Earls. A shadow of Oxford's fancy about Leycester may be glimpsed in the refusal of Claudius to let his nephew go back to the university in Wittenberg. The King wants to keep Hamlet always under his eye. The dramatist's illusion about Leycester's interest in him repeated psychic history. Claudius stands not only for De Vere's rival Dudley but also for his stepfather Tyrrell, his imaginary rival in boyhood, the lover of his mother. Oxford in early youth probably fabricated many a daydream in which Tyrrell plotted to rob him of Castle Hedingham and the rest of the Vere domains by cunningly cutting short his life. We have poetic testimony of the terror that his stepfather provoked in the personage of Tyrrell, the murderer of the boy prince Edward in Shakespeare's *Richard III.*

The character of the Danish monarch, in my belief, is a trinity. He embodies together with the poet's conceptions of Dudley and Tyrrell his idea of the tyranny of John de Vere, his father. Viscount Bulbeck, the child Edward de Vere, trembled in fear of Lord John, whom he surely viewed as a criminal long before he learnt about the charges of the Duke of Somerset. The immense price that his father was willing to pay to escape condemnation for those charges proves they included treason and homicide. Infant impressions of Lord John's amorous temper were confirmed when his son discovered how careless John was in getting married the second time, so that his eldest daughter, Katherine, was convinced all her life that her half-brother Edward and his sister Mary were actually bastards. The court scandal-mongers would not have left Edward in ignorance of his father's affair with Mistress Dorothy, the servant of Katherine's mother. So the poet had sufficient information and fiction to enable him to think of his father as a secret adulterer and assassin, quite capable of castrating him.

The image of Margery Golding, as I tried to prove in my study of the *Comedy of Errors*, formed the nucleus of the dramatist's superego. But it was overshadowed by the idol he called father. The Lord John he introjected in his juvenile years became his god, distorted a little to look more like himself. Little Viscount Bulbeck was familiar with the ego's mechanism for protection against anxiety, the petcock known as identification with the aggressor, which turned into an engine of his political creed. The mechanism broke down under the fighting in his mind between the mother-goddess and the father-god. He had not the heart to combat them both, and in his forcible-feeble way he loved them. Love and dread of his father compelled him to give up his child-claim to a carnal monopoly of her. But instead of going to hunt a love that would take the mother's place in his heart, he prostrated himself before the mental idol of her mate. He strove to disarm the god by renouncing his birthright of masculine integrity; in his soul's oblivion he unsexed himself. To make sure of his father's good will and to restore peace in his ego, the child desired to be ravished by Earl John, in the way he imagined his mother was raped. The real John, however, would never allow his son to fawn and cling on him, to be girlishly servile, in short, to seduce him. His Lordship ironly insisted that Bulbeck play the man. The memory of his rebukes and the terror of mutilation and death at his father's hands completed the foundation of derangement in the boy's brain. From then on, wherever he saw and heard someone denouncing his effeminacy or exhorting him to act like a man, the love which he radiated toward militant males rushed back into his unconscious to balm his pride and nourish his narcissism. Self-pity and self-derision would often drive it out again, with flare-ups of hysteria, crying to be welcomed and liked. Therefore when the guards of Elsinore take leave of Hamlet with the polite words, "Our duty to your honor," the Prince replies, not without pathos, "Your loves, as mine to you." In the chaos of his conscience there was rarely sustained repose for his sexual energy.

From the state of self-pity, familiar to Shakespeare under the name of melancholy, he was able again and again to rise with renewed youth to the peaks of creative labor where he wrote his songs, sonnets and plays. I have endeavored to chart the process or the path of his ascent. Before he entered the stage of self-pity, he apparently endured a period of misery when he consented to the judgment of his enemies and almost despised himself. This inward aggression would soon submerge in the tide of inward libido and alter to pity, softening the chastisement of his superego. Then the superego itself softened. The poet passed into a trance where the mother within, laved by libido, turned from an image of mythic horror into one secreting the milk of human kindness. In a word, he mothered himself. The process amounts to a truce between superego and id, a condition which allows resurgence of the infant illusion of almightiness and gives rise to the faith that can add cubits to human stature and nearly work miracles. (Edmund Bergler termed a similar performance of narcissism "the autarchic fantasy," and interpreted it differently. [Cp. *The Writer and Psychoanalysis*, 1949, chapter iii.] In Bergler's notion of the superego there is no room for libidinal transformation of conscience.) This truce of mutual compassion between the two chief powers of the spirit liberated the artist temporarily from his distresses and fears. However his enjoyment of the mood, childlike, magical, could not last. It made him blush perceiving the womanly elements in his mind. The father within would make cruel mirth at him, and the unity with the maternal would end. In the separation he would assert the wholeness and indomitability of his phallic self, and reach for the pen, that symbol of his sex, to uplift and justify his pride. He conquered the anguish of his internal war, which threatened disintegration of his ego, by producing a new cosmos of his own out of paper and into making his little playworld fruitful by lavishing upon it invisible seed. In this operation he was not pretending paternity. He was still mothering himself. The fantastic seed he distributed, in the oblivion of his genius, meant milk. Only when the spell of creation finished, when he had rehearsed his perplexities and excused his sins at home, in the empire of his pen,—only then could he have the luxury of feeling reconciled to the paternal demon in his head, and so dare to engage in games of fatherhood. He became a father in the theater. He planted his seed on the stage, fostered groups of players and playwrights, and in the interludes of dreamlike life among these peripheral boyish people considered himself in truth an uncrowned king.

When I wrote this interpretation of Shakespeare's fatherhood in literature, the idea struck me gently that his unconscious tenacity to the thoughts of semen and milk worked to protect him from the dismal notion of a thing these fluids represented in his id. What could this terrible object be? I could only guess, on the basis of my belief that the artist lived in perpetual head-long flight from the wish for feminine subjection to the men who reminded him profoundly of his father. My conjecture therefore counterposed to his cherished fancies of the two body liquids the image of something solid symbolic of both parents—an object standing for his concept of paternal rape and visions of his mother as consoler and poisoner, fountain of life and death.

What else but the phallus, the fetish of his entire life, which he flaunted in his very pen-name? The male member, since his first hour of masturbation, had always been for him a thing of fascination and fear, terrible as an army with pennants, because it suggested the challenge of his father and the mystery of his mother. By autoerotic traumaturgy he united his mental image of the organ with the ever-coveted maternal nipple, which our

Shakespeare's beginning greed and early maternal punishment had nearly made a Dead Sea fruit for him. The dramatist gave us an unforgettable charade of this cult of his oblivion in the scene where Hamlet talks about the heart of his mystery while fingering the melodious pipe.

The primary *Hamlet* appears to have been written in a blaze of hysteria, when the dramatist struggled to persuade himself that he was a man of action, eager to crush his foes, and courageous enough to tell Queen Elizabeth the truth. His second treatment of the story may be described as an interlude of obsessional counterattack, marking a desperate religious effort to escape the ravages of his real disease. Finally he rewrote the drama as if with the deliberate intention to portray the malady of his soul, to understand himself. In his old age, verily on the verge of extinction by one of London's periodic plagues, he made the tragedy a revelation of narcissic fury and folly that should have encouraged the creation of a true science of memory (psychology) centuries ago.

Perhaps a critic will inquire: If the Prince of Denmark is so pathetic a specimen of mankind as you have drawn here, why has he captivated the intelligence of ages and traversed the continents with more admiration than any other character in world literature?

I trust that my concentration on the Prince's pathology will not lead any reader to lose sight of the merits that have earned him his unequalled praise. We all realize the play awards us the portrait of a genius, in many respects the world's paramount artist, nearly at full length. Hamlet was the first of Shakespeare's major dramas in which he came close to baring the ordeals of his powerfully gifted, extremely perceptive ego, the lures to delirium and gloom abysmal, the raptures and excruciations, he had to endure in his solitary battle for sanity. I have outlined the more energetic rescue devices he employed with the brilliance we would anticipate from a man of his choice culture and heredity. In particular I propose that we examine that delicate combination of instruments called Hamlet's sense of humor, in the light of the poet's defiance of perils, both external and instinctual, perils he could laugh at after he no longer feared them. Far be it from me to underestimate the scope and force of Hamlet's wit, the skeptic acid of his irony. But the intellect of the sad Dane had been well surveyed by other analysts, and the strength of his laughter is a permanent part of the race's arsenal for dealing with our troubles and problems.

Two attainments of Hamlet's wisdom I would like to stress: his cosmopolitan scope, and his discernment of the new social order evolving in the shell of perishing feudalism during the dramatist's lifetime.

The international vision of Hamlet is the faculty that raised his creator to the magnitude of a true father of his country. For by his terrestrial outlook and insight he was emboldened to compare his people's accomplishments and shortcomings with those of foreign lands, and inform England of what he had learnt. In this way he contributed mightily to the education, the upbringing of his countrymen. For instance, Shakespeare pronounces from the mouth of Hamlet a verdict against the Danish habit of drinking to boordom. However the sober listener to his speech among the English would recognize at once an exposure of bad manners in their own land. Shakespeare repeated the criticism in *Othello*, aiming it directly at England. The comment of his grave-digging clown on the craziness of the English could be taken as a joke. Yet there was more than clowning in his denuding of the zeal with which England, unquestioning, doggedly faithful, obeys the orders alleged to come from King Claudius and beheads his two innocent envoys. The last laugh in the tragedy, when the English ambassadors arrive to report, "too late," what good errand-runners they are, and wonder "Where should we have our thanks?" conveys a lesson to patriots.

From the loins of a great lover of his country descended the soldier, scholar, and parliamentarian Sir Edward Vere, who gave his life to help break the Spanish empire at the time when his king's chief minister, Sir Robert Cecil, was privately conspiring to redeem the Spaniards from the costs of war. And a descendant of cousin Horatio, Lady Anne Vere Fairfax, assisted in the overthrow of the English monarchy and bravely stood up against Oliver Cromwell and his comrades when they craved King Charles's blood. The lives of these fighting Veres illustrate the main lessons of *Hamlet.*

To the cosmopolitan scope of *Hamlet* and various personal sorrows of Shakespeare we owe the drama's apprehension of the great changes that church and state were undergoing in Europe in the sixteenth century. The poet was bound to be hostile to the revolutionary Puritans. They appeared to him ludicrous upstarts, who wished to try out in statecraft the measures and delusions of their handicraft. He burlesqued them in his spectacle of the sexton-buffoon who preaches the democratic dogma of the "even Christian," namely the conviction that a common Christian sinner is equally as valuable in the scales of God as any other child of the Church. By the tongue of the comedian he made fun of the kindred faith preached by Father John Ball and his fellow insurgents in the age of Chaucer:

> When Adam dolve and Eve span,
> Who was then the gentleman?

The Clown declares, "There is no ancient gentlemen but gardeners…they hold up Adam's profession." Shakespeare believed that Adam's profession might be noble in the wilderness but civilization required the subordination of gardeners to gentlemen with cleaner and more crucial occupations. All men are created unequal, he thought, and are destined by celestial law to govern or to serve. He absolutely rejected the belief of Burghley that "gentility is nothing but ancient riches." Riches not designed for ornament and graciousness were hardly better than dirt in our poet's opinion. To his way of thinking, gentility signified virtue, and virtue meant venerable stock, an old holiness of blood. The structure of society best fitted to do the will of God with this blood was, of course, the framework of feudalism. Against the foes of feudalism who worked with rough hands and homespun reason, the dramatist would not condescend to use a weapon sharper than hearty laughter. But he hated the enemies of feudalism who fought with money and cunning. He hated the masters of the middle class, the Cecils, Bacons, Hattons, in whose theology and politics he spied an evil energy capable of disintegrating the chivalry, the lordliness, the social differences he held dear. To combat them De Vere had joined the party of the ancient aristocracy headed by the Howards. But then he discovered the low esteem in which this party held him. He learnt that their creed did not exclude the pursuit of money for state secrets and possibly the sale of their country to Rome or Spain. "The Howards," he proclaimed, "were the most treacherous race under heaven."[97] The shock of this disclosure concerning his noble kin left him intensely aware of the failure of virtue in the Veres, specifically himself. "What should such fellows as I do crawling between heaven and earth?" Hamlet's honesty in the question allows us to observe the thoughts his author was harboring about his own gentility. The whole play is the product of Shakespeare's angry meditations on the rottenness which he had detected in royalty. He saw the divinity around the throne of Elizabeth as no better than the religion of Claudius. The King did not share the medieval prejudice for leaving killers in peace when they took refuge in a sanctuary. He approves the eagerness of Laertes to cut Hamlet's throat in the church. Queen Elizabeth was no less broadminded in affairs of political homicide. She could seldom be blamed for Quixotic clemency. Relentless in hanging Puritans, burning Anabaptists, racking and butchering Catholics, she reduced Christianity to a tool of state. She also reduced chivalry to its original meaning of horsemanship, and confined it to tournaments. From the year 1580, when our dramatist began to examine these phenomena in earnest, he was driven to acknowledge that the medieval code of his youth had more castles in the air than on earth. With his loss of faith in feudal standards, and continuing hatred of the bourgeois undertakers seeking to bury the old system, he found himself mentally isolated, an outcast from society. New friends peered out from the underworld dregs of civilization, the gutter proletariat's exemplars of humanity beyond his wildest dreams.

Emerging from the exile, still ethically alone, he rewrote *Hamlet*. He sang farewell to the ideals of his father and poured out his contempt for the economic cult of the future. The former he consigned to the dust of an impotent wintry ghost, and the cult of capital he damned to Osric's dirt and the clay where his clowns put Polonius. The reflection hurt him that the glorious bodies of Alexander and Caesar—not to mention saints and knights—might have gone a worse way. For a while he tried to retain the youthful confidence of his letter to Thomas Bedingfield preluding *Cardanus' Comfort*, in which he chanted: "For when all things shall else forsake us, virtue will ever abide with us, and when our bodies fall into the bowels of the earth, yet that shall mount with our minds into the highest heavens."[98] When he reached the final cadences of *Hamlet* and listened to the music of his adolescent fidelity in Horatio's epiphany of flights of angels singing the Prince to rest, he heard nothing more holy than a lullaby.

Deep in the dramatist's mind, naturally, there sparkled inextinguishable the belief of life in its own immortality, and the singular readiness of Edward de Vere for the new and adventurous in thought. He embraced the idea of dreaming after death. No matter how hard he found it to grant human beings admission to the sanctuary of his soul, he always had plenty of warm corners for their inquiries into nature and history, their theories and their whims. This peculiarity of withdrawing from men while opening his arms to their guesswork and dreams—"airy nothing"—is in rhythm with the unconscious pulse of philosophy, which Freud related to the paranoiac architecture.

> The neuroses exhibit on one hand striking and far-reaching points of agreement with those great social constructions, art, religion and philosophy. But on the other hand they seem like distortions of them. It might be maintained that a case of hysteria is a caricature of art-work, that an obsessional neurosis is a caricature of a religion, and that a paranoic delusion is a caricature of a philosophic system.[99]

At all events, the intellectual hospitality of Hamlet endears him to us perhaps more than any other trait. He saved himself from madness, from utter estrangement from humanity, by his passionate curiosity for the strange, his affection for innovators and outcasts, living anachronisms and too early dying pioneers, the fellows whom he unconsciously regarded as brother-figures and sons. Is there a line in his drama more delightful than Hamlet's answer to Horatio when his friend, dismayed by the voice of the Ghost (a cryptic echo of the Prince), cries out, "O day and night, but this is wondrous strange!"

And therefore as a stranger give it welcome.

****

Epilog

When Hamlet assures the two lads who were "of so young days brought up with him," that "there is nothing either good or bad, but thinking makes it so," his brains were vibrating with the skeptic standpoint of Michel de Montaigne, whose writings appear to have pleased him as the most Promethean, fire-fetching, or Luciferian, light-lifting, literature coming out of Europe. I have traced his statement however to its immediate source in the classic probe of rationality by Sextus Empiricus. We learn from the preface to Philip Sidney's *Astrophel and Stella,* which the Earl of Oxford's comic companion Thomas Nash arranged for printing and dispatched on June 1, 1591, that the works of Sextus Empiricus had been lately translated into English. But no edition has been located to the present date. Nash delivered a single gem from the works: "our opinion (as Sextus Empiricus affirmeth) gives the name of good or ill to everything." Exactly Shakespeare's quotation.

Nash liked to rap imaginary knuckles of critics who scoured his books for concealed allusions to cruxes or scandals of the ruling class. For example, in his Prolog to Summer's *Last Will and Testament* (1592) he demands: "Moralizers, you that wrest a never meant meaning out of every thing, applying all things to the present time, keep your attention for the common Stage: for here are no quips in characters for you to read...Spite, spell backwards what thou canst." Courtiers and educated gentry of the age found endless titillation in the practice of translating the terminology of current political and theological scriptures, above all, it seems, the references to church and state made on the stage, in search of secrets. In fact Queen Bess led the nation in this detective practice too. Burghley, practically her prime minister, bears witness to her skill in a letter to his son Robert, dated December 7, 1593, intended for her Majesty's eyes. He speaks of "my former allegorical letter written to you, in which I perceive her Majesty discovered the literal sense thereof before the midst of it seen. I must confess that my cunning therein was not sufficient to hide the sense from her Majesty, though I think never a lady besides her, nor a decipherer in the Court, would have dissolved the figure to have found the sense as her Majesty hath done…I did it rather to make her some sport."[100]

Shakespeare had queenly precedent in calling Burghley, in the person of Polonius, a tedious old fool. Elizabeth once denounced her Treasurer as "a forward old fool." About the same time, 1596, Robert Devereux the Earl of Essex, Leycester's political lieutenant, was fond of referring to Burghley as the fox. Yet Essex told the Queen the unadorned truth when he assured her that William Cecil was "the greatest, gravest, and most esteemed Councilor your Majesty ever had."[101]

In July 1597 a peppery Polonius arrived from Poland to rebuke the Queen for claiming maritime superiority on the Atlantic and producing havoc in Spanish commerce with his king Sigismund. The envoy's name was Paulus. He talked to Elizabeth in Latin; she had to answer him in the same language. "God's death, my lords!" she swore to her courtiers, "I have been enforced this day to scour up my old Latin, that hath long lain rusting." For a fortnight Burghley had to busy himself with Polish affairs. His son-in-law, faithful to his calling, a spy of God, observed the diplomacy and clandestine dealing with his unique twinklers. "The Polak has troubled us here," one of Burghley's secretaries complained. But the business ultimately meant only grist for the Hamlet mill.[102]

Something which would have interested our dramatist far more was the Queen's curiosity about incest in high places.

On November 13, 1597, she summoned Sir John Fortescue and Robert Cecil to get her the facts about certain horrible incestuous marriages she had heard about, said to have been made by "Commons." Unluckily the chronicles of the Queen yield no more information about the mischief.

In 1599 an obscure scribbler named Richard Johnson printed a romance entitled *The Most Pleasant History of Tom o Lincoln the Red Rose Knight*, which augments the testimony that *Hamlet* already exerted a dynamic influence on English mentality. Just listen to part of its plot: The hero's father returns from the region of Pluto to command his son, "revenge my death upon thy adulterous mother; thy mother now living in the filthiness of shame, making the castle where she now remains in, a lustful stews; there was I murthered, and there buried in a stinking dung-hill; no man gave me funeral tears, nor any sorrowed for my death; I that have dared death in the face, and purchast honour in many kingdoms, was slain by my own wife, by my nearest friend, by my second self, by Anglitora, by her whom the whole world admired for virtue… Rise, I say, and let the pavements of that castle be sprinkled with their detested blood, the blood of the monster that hath not only despoiled my marriage bed of honoured dignities, but like a tyrant to her own flesh hath murthered me." The ghost tells his son where he wants his blade driven: "wound thy cursed mother's breast."[103] Gilbert Murray might have found this stuff useful for his argument (in June 1914) that the malady of Hamlet was rooted in wrath toward his mother more than toward her lover.[104]

If Shakespeare composed the most recited of his soliloquies during a season of dietary and perhaps sexual abstinence, then my suspicion that he wrote it with a particular passage from Boccaccio chuckling compulsively in his skull may have good enough ground to uphold it here. There is a tale in the *Decameron* where an aged judge argues or pleads with his wife that they should refrain from carnal embraces on saints day, thru Lent, and so on—"thinking perhaps that there should be the same delays with women in bed as he often arranged in lawsuits."[105] The grim joke may have struck our dramatist, whose experience with courts, especially their entanglements over the fee simple or complex tenancy of his estates, occasionally became harrowing, as providing a motive for suicide. He coupled in one line the same concepts that aroused Boccaccio's hilarity because they tormented him: "The pangs of despis'd love, the law's delay..."

Of course the life-erosion of the courts reminded him instantly of "The insolence of office," the daily cruelties of politics, distinguisht from "The oppressor's wrong" by their quotidian commonplace drudgery. These phrases recalled for me an aspect of Tudor statecraft that the poet mentions in the last act of his play, in lines that I value as an odd bit of autobiography:

> I once did hold it, as our statists do,
> A baseness to write fair, and labour'd much
> How to forget that learning... (Act V, Scene 2)

Anyone who has scrutinized the script of a politician like Charles Arundel will understand at once what Hamlet meant. Arundel's aversion to writing intelligibly is manifest on every page he produced. Eras before Talleyrand, he was persuaded that language was invented to hide thought, at least writing must have been. The appalling futility of his penmanship becomes ludicrous in contrast with the mature script of the Earl of Oxford, whose pages are a pleasure to read. They shine with his steady aspiration to clarity, often rising to a rare calligraphy.

In 1600 the sullen satirist John Marston wrote for the children of Paul's Cathedral a comedy named *Jack Drum's Entertainment.* He points out in the first pages that he made the comedy when peace was being debated with Spain, in a "woman's year," that is a leap year. It was registered for printing in 1601, evidently after a short season at the Blackfriars theater. These children of the Cathedral quire were the same little actors mentioned in *Hamlet* as winning fashion-fame with plays that Ben Jonson sneered at on account of their age. "I saw the children of Pauls last night," pipes the opening speech in Marston's comedy. "...The apes, in time, will do it handsomely." Even tho, it must be confest, they produce

> Such musty fopperies of antiquity,
> And do not suit the humorous age's backs
> With clothes in fashion. (Act V, Scene 3)

There is but one character in the comedy who scintillates with life today, a knight whose dominant note is one of lamentation over the decline of aristocracy and the upsurge of burgess impudence. His name is Sir Edward Fortune, and thus runs his theme-song:

> Each Cobler's spawn, and yeasty, boozing bench,
> Reeks in the face of sacred majesty
> His stinking breath of censure! (Act I, Scene 1)

Sir Edward ridicules the Commons, who dare like the satirist,

> Discourse as confident of peace with Spain,
> As if the Genius of quick Machiavel
> Usher'd his speech!

The youngster Ned Planet, who loves one of Sir Edward's daughters, Camelia, promises to resemble her father in this manner: "now I'l be as sociable as Timon of Athens" (Act II). Sir Edward Fortune, with Lord Edward de Vere, worries over his girls' future: "I do love my Girls should wish me live, Which few o wish that have a greedy Sire." (Act I, Scene 1) He himself refuses to live like a courtier, and urges his daughters to choose their husbands in freedom of love—while keeping an eye open to the advantages of widowers.

In August 1601 came the gloomy news that Francis Vere had been wounded severely in the head at the siege of Ostend. Count Maurice of Nassau bewildered and amused his English colleagues in the war with his technology of tunnels and trenches. Shakespeare must have been often regaled with anecdotes of the Dutchman's fierce fondness for machinery, and his search of brand new devices "to terrace himself in the earth like a mole."[106] What else was the dramatist thinking of when he presented the "buried majesty of Denmark" under the mockery of being called "old mole" and "worthy pioneer"?

Toward the close of February 1601 Robert Devereux, Earl of Essex, suffered on the scaffold for having trusted Lord Henry Howard and failing to understand the soul of Robert Cecil, both of whom desired patiently and long the Earl's bloody death. An unknown bard, loyal to the house of Leycester, seems to have grieved over the execution of Essex in verse, which he dared not print however until 1606. In that year W. H., Gent. (perhaps William Herbert of Glamorgan?) let the world have his *Englands Sorrow or A Farewell to Essex*. After a loving description of his hero—"Grace made him great, and greatness threw him down"—the poet suddenly applauded Devereux's relative Sir Philip Sidney, and remembered the martyred knight with lines that would have reminded the friends and foes of Sidney immediately of his rivalry in rime with Lord Edward de Vere.

> "Thou wert a man yborn to govern men
> And hadst thou lived thou mightst have bin a King."

Many an Englishman could recall Edmund Spenser's endeavor in his *Shepherd's Calendar to* make peace between Oxford and

Sidney after the latter had despatched his ridiculous reply to the Earl's epigram, "Were I a king," in which Philip warned his antagonist,

> "Wert thou a king, ye'd not command content,
> Sith empire none thy mind could yet suffice."

In a marginal note in *Englands Sorrow* W. H. reported that Sidney had once been deemed deserving of exaltation to the throne of Poland: "Some say he should have been elected King of Poland: it is most certain, he was well esteemed of all the Vaybodes (barons), at his being in that Kingdom."[108] Philip was a guest of Poland in the autumn of 1574. The Earl of Oxford may have heard a legend of his being considered for the crown of the Poles, and experienced a sting of envy which eventually could have contributed to the final lines of *Hamlet* the sad assurance that our hero was worthy of being elected a king. Yet none knew better than Hamlet's creator that poor Sidney had told him the truth when he wrote: "empire none thy mind could yet suffice." How could he narrow his brains to a realm of wormy marl? He, the artist whom Alexandre Dumas (the father) proclaimed: After God, he created the most.

The period of the first publications of *Hamlet* saw the author's actors, the Lord Chamberlain's company, suffering from restricted income at all their playhouses, metropolitan and provincial. "The records of 1603-16 show that the Company traveled in most of these years, and that there were long periods of inhibition, chiefly for plague, during which the meagre profits of provincial performances and the royal allowances for private practice would be a poor compensation for the closure of the London houses."[107] Late in 1603 a pair of unimportant printers gave the world *The Tragical History of Hamlet, Prince of Denmark*, by William Shakespeare. They promised their customers the play was exactly as performed "by his Highness' servants" in London, at "the two Universities," and elsewhere.

The Lord Chamberlain's men became King James's servants soon after he took Elizabeth's throne. This may be the reason for the appearance of the royal coat of arms on the second quarto, "the true and perfect copy" of our tragedy. Yet there may be an ulterior reason, a molecular insinuation of the writer, who prepared the drama for the press while he felt himself getting ready bodily for the commonwealth of moles and worms. Edward de Vere, Earl of Oxford, died on June 24, 1604, in his residence called "King's Place," leaving no will nor testament. Twelve days later, his widow, his son Henry, who inherited the earldom, and died a hero in the Dutch republic's war against Spain, and probably his noble bastard who won glory as the mysterious Sir Edward Vere, buried the king of English theater and literature.[108]

Hindnotes

1 Freud, *Complete Psychological Works* (London 1953) 12, 266n.
2 Freud, *Outline of Psychoanalysis* (New York 1949) 96.
3 Jones, *Hamlet and Oedipus* (London 1949) 112n.
4 G. Harvey, *Marginalia*, ed. Moore Smith (Stratford 1913) 232.
5 *Shakspere Allusion Book*, ed. Munro (London 1932) I, 29.
6 *Diary of Philip Henslowe*, ed. Collier (London 1845) 35.
7 Harvey, *Works*, ed. Grosart (London 1884) i. 273.
8 Jones, op. cit. 106. See F.S. Boas, ed. *The Works of Thomas Kyd* (Oxford 1901) xlv, liv.
9 Nash, *Works*, ed. McKerrow (London 1910) iii, 316.
10 A.B. Grosart, ed. *Works of Robert Greene* (London 1883) vi, 288.
11 M.B. Evans, *Der bestrafte Brudermord; sein Verhaeltnis zu Shakspeares Hamlet* (Hamburg 1910) 23.
12 A.S. Cairncross, *The Problem of Hamlet; a Solution* (London 1936).
13 V. Courdaveaux (1867) quoted in the Variorum edition of *Hamlet*, ed. Furness (Philadelphia 1877) ii, 389.
14 *Diary of Henry Machyn*, ed. Nicholas (London 1848) 290. *Harleian Ms.* 897, f. 81. *Calendar of Hastings Manuscripts*, I, 319. State Papers Foreign (1561-62) 103.
15 *Lansdowne Ms.* 6, art. 20.
16 *Calendar of Proceedings in Chancery*, G/g 7, no. 34.
17 F. Chancellor, *The ancient sepulchral monuments of Essex* (London 1890) 161.

18 Acts of the Privy Council, ed. Dansent, iv, 305. *Calendar of State Papers Domestic* (1554) ii, 4; iii, 4.

19 John Strype, *Annals of the Reformation* (London 1731) I, 36.

20 *State Papers Domestic* (1581) cli, 46. (Public Record Office, London).

21 J.A. Froude, *History of England* (London 1865) I, 75. C. Read, *Mr. Secretary Cecil* (New York 1955) 214. J.D. Wilson, *The Essential Shakespeare* (London 1932) 104.

22 Read, *Cecil*, 212-16, 227. *State Papers Domestic* (1561) xix, 26; xx, 20, 41; idem (1562) xxii, 17, 49; xxiii, 24.

23 *Calendar of Cecil* (Salisbury) *Ms.* at Hatfield, ii. 144.

24 *State Papers Domestic* (1563) xxvii, 71. Read, op. cit. 79.

25 Allen, *The Life Story of Edward de Vere as "William Shakespeare"* (London 1932) 203.

26 *State Papers Domestic* (1559) vii, 2, 5, 72. *State Papers Foreign* (1559) 5. Strype, op. cit. i, 195. John Stow, *The Annals of England* (London 1580) 34.

26a *Calendar of Cecil Ms.* xiii, 381. Ellis, *My Life* (Boston 1939) 414.

27 Read, op. cit. 273, 282. Strype, op cit. i, 357.

28 Read, 306, 307.

29 Ibid. 212.

30 *State Papers Domestic* (1565) xxxvi, 66. Strype, op. cit. i, 515. Brandes, *William Shakespeare* (London 1924) 364.

31 *State Papers*, ed. Murdin (London 1759) 764. Cecil Ms. ii, 171.

32 *State Papers Domestic* (1581) cli, 44, 45.

33 Strype, *Annals*, iii, 60; ii, 121. Read, op cit. 436. Cecil Ms. I, 415.

34 *Calendar of Rutland Ms.* i, 94, 95.

35 Read, *Cecil*, 309.

36 *Huntington Library Bulletin* (1946) no. 6, 17.

37 B.M. Ward, *The Seventeenth Earl of Oxford* (London 1928) 66. Harleian Ms. 6991, f. 9. Lansdowne Ms. 14:85. Cecil Ms. xiv, 19; ii, 68.

38 Edmund Lodge, *Illustrations of British History* (London 1838) ii, 17. Cp. Bronson Feldman, "Helen of Rose-Ilion," *Secrets of Shakespeare* (Philadelphia 1972) 21-71.

39 Cecil Ms. ii, 83.

40 *State Papers Foreign* (1576) no. 735, 799. Ward, *Oxford*, 118; Allen, op. cit. 67.

41 Feldman, "Imaginary Incest," *American Imago*, 12 (Summer 1955) 117.

42 *State Papers Foreign* (1577) 349, 350.

43 Edgar Fripp, *Shakespeare: Man and Artist* (Oxford 1938) i, 146-7.

44 *The Fugger News Letters*, Second Series, ed. Klarwill (New York 1926) 59.

45 Lansdowne Ms. 39:22.

46 Sir Nicholas Harris Nicolas, *Memoirs of the Life and Times of Sir Christopher Hatton* (London 1847) 321-4, 497.

47 *The Shakespeare Fellowship News Letter* (London, March 1947) 5.

48 Rutland Ms. i, 150. Lansdowne Ms. 39:42.

49 R. Naunton, *Fragmenta Regalia*, ed. Arber (London 1870) 30. *History of Queen Elizabeth, Amy Robsart and the Earl of Leicester*, ed. Burgoyne (London 1904), 38, 44.

50 Harvey, *Gratulationes Valdinenses* (1578), Latin oration for Lord Burghley.

51 Lansdowne Ms. 38:62.

52 Nicolas, op. cit. 345-6. E.M. Tenison, *Elizabethan England* (Leamington 1935) v, 76.

53 *The Fugger News Letters*, Second Series, 81-2, 83.

54 C.W. Barrell, "New Milestone in Shakespearean Research," *The Shakespeare Fellowship Quarterly*, V (October 1944) 57, 62.

55 *Sayings of Queen Elizabeth*, ed. Chamberlin (London 1923) 158.

56 Lansdowne Ms. 99:93. *State Papers Domestic* (1584) cixvii, 16.

57 V. Von Klarwill, ed. *Queen Elizabeth and Some Foreigners* (New York 1928) 332.

58 *State Papers Domestic* (1581) cli, 43, 44, 49, 50, 57. Public Record Office (London 1563): Wards, 8, 13, f. 521; quoted by Gwynneth Bowen, in the *Shakespearean Authorship Review*, No. 24 (1971).

59 Looney, *Shakespeare Identified* (London 1920) 408. Fuller, *Worthies of England*, ed. Nuttall (London 1840) i, 514.

60 Allen, op. cit. 3.

61 Lansdowne Ms. 99:93. Talbot Ms. G, 250.

62 W.H. Widgery, *The First Quarto Edition of Hamlet* (Cambridge 1880).

62a Greene, *Works*, ed. Grosart, v, 69, 103. W. Whiter, *A Specimen of a Commentary on Shakespeare* (London 1794) ed. *Over Bell* (London 1967) 123-7; C.F. Spurgeon, *Shakespeare's Imagery, and What It Tells Us* (London 1935) 195-9.

63 Strype, *Annals*, iv, 342.

64 Froude, op. cit. xi, 579. *Fugger News Letters*, Second Series, 186.

65 A. Acheson, *Shakespeare, Chapman, and Thomas More* (London 1931) 46.

65a Feldman, "Shakespeare's Jester—Oxford's Servant," *Shakespeare Fellowship Quarterly*, viii (Autumn 1947).

66 Froude, *History of England*, xii, 75.

67 Feldman, "Othello in Reality," *American Imago*, 11 (Summer 1954).

68 A. Hart, "The Date of Othello," *London Times Literary Supplement* (October 10, 1935) 631.

69 Harleian Ms. 286, f. 102.

70 Lansdowne Ms. 103:38.

71 Manuscripts of the Earl of Ancaster, 137, 156.
71a Ward, *Oxford*, 289, 292.
72 Edmund Bohann, *The Character of Queen Elizabeth* (London 1693) 341.
73 Barrell, op. cit 53, 55, 57.
74 Froude, op. cit. xi, 579. *Fugger News Letters*, Second Series, 186.
75 Nash, *Works*, ed. McKerrow, vi, 80.
76 Ward, op. cit. 286.
76a Calendar of Penshurst Ms. ii, 184.
77 Sir Richard Phillips in *The Monthly Magazine or British Register*, xiv (1818); E.K. Chambers, *William Shakespeare: Facts and Problems* (Oxford, 1930) ii, 299.
78 Feldman, "Shakespeare's Jester," loc. cit. 41.
79 J.L. Motley, *History of the United Netherlands* (New York 1868) iv, 36.
80 Francis Vere, *Commentaries*, ed. Dillingham (Cambridge 1657) 129.
81 Lodge, *British History*, i, 449n.
82 Burgoyne, ed. *History of Queen Elizabeth*, 49.
82a J.H. Pollen, *The Earl of Arundel* (Catholic Record Society, xxi) 58, 66.
83 Philip Morant, *The History and Antiquities of Essex* (London 1768) ii, 293n.
84 F.S. Boas, *University Drama in the Tudor Age* (Oxford 1914) 166, 180.
84a *Variorum of Hamlet*, ed. Furness, ii. 187.
85 *State Papers Domestic* (1581) cli, 44.
85a Feldman, "Imaginary Incest," *American Imago*, 12 (Summer 1955).
86 *Standard Dictionary of Folklore, Mythology, and Legend*, ed. Leash and Fried (New York 1950) ii, 838.
87 *Variorum*, i, 333; ii, 161, 162.

88 Ibid. ii, 147. Madariaga, *On Hamlet* (London 1948) 105. Cp. Karl Rosner, *Shakespeares Hamlet im Lichte der Neuropathologie* (Berlin 1895).

89 Freud, *Collected Papers* (London 1924) iii, 390f. No examination of the Schreber problem would be adequate without a perusal of the criticism of Freud's interpretation by Ida Macalpine and her son Richard Hunter. I favor their view. See note 91.

90 Tucker Brooke, *Life of Christopher Marlowe* (New York 1930) 104. Calendar of State Papers, Ireland (October 1587) 424.

91 Daniel Paul Schreber, *Memoirs of My Nervous Illness*, ed. Macalpine and Hunter (London 1955); above all the "Discussion," 372f.

92 K. Malone, "Further Etymologies for Hamlet," *Review of English Studies*, iv (July 1928) 257.

93 Ward, op. cit. 193.

94 *State Papers Domestic* (1581) cli, 57.

95 Chateaubriand, *Sketches of English Literature* (London 1837) ii, 313.

96 *State Papers Domestic* (1581) cli, 46.

97 *State Papers Domestic* (1581) cli, 45. Froude, op. cit. xi, 518n.

98 *Poems of Edward de Vere*, ed. Looney (London 1921) 20.

99 Freud, *Totem and Taboo* (Vienna 1913), tr. Strachey (London 1954) i, 448.

100 Francis Peck, *Desiderata Curiosa* (London 1735) v, 2.

101 Thomas Birch, *Memoirs of the Reign of Queen Elizabeth* (London 1754) i, 448.

102 Read, *Lord Burghley and Queen Elizabeth* (New York 1960) 529.

103 *From Early English Prose Romances*, ed. Thoms (London 1907) 601-690.

104 Murray, "Hamlet and Orestes: A Study in Traditional Types," *Proceedings of the British Academy*, 1914. Dr.

Fredric Wertham developed Murray's argument on the Orestes complex in his *Dark Legend* (New York 1941).

105 Boccaccio, *Decameron*, tr. Aldington (Garden City 1930) 128.

106 Calendar of Cecil Ms. xi, 308.

107 E.K. Chambers, op. cit. ii, 70.

108 Tenison, *Elizabethan England*, xii, 414, 415.

Inquisition

Not long after the completion of my monograph on *Hamlet*, I managed to afford the services of a London scribe, whom I was able to guide, by mail, to the British Public Record Office document containing the coroners inquest on the sanguine death of Thomas Brinknell in July 1567 at the hand of Edward de Vere. The following transcription of the inquest text informs us of all that we will probably ever learn about the homicide.

KB. 9/619

Inquisiciio indentata capta apud St martynes in campis in comitatu xxijto die Julii anno regni Elizabeth deo gratia Angl', Franc', Hib(er)n' Regine fidei defensor etc. nono, coram R(icar) do Vale uno coron (ario) dicte d'e (domine) Regine in com' (comitatu) predicto super visum corporis Thome Brinckenell', nuper de civitate Westm' in comitatu pre(dic)te yoman ib(ide) m iacentis mortui per sacrum Johanis Martyne, Willelmi Waters, Anthonii Harris, Johanis Whitehedd, Willelmi Beseley, Humfridi Mote, Johanis Toyher, Johanis Baves, Willelmi Fletcher, Randolphi Holynshedd, Johnis Bagleyne, Thome Sedon, Georgii Hedges, Jacobi Seward, Willelmi Wakefeld,, jacobi Pykes et Roberti Bottell, proborum et legalum hminum de comitatu predicto qui dicunt super sacrum suum quod ubi vicesimo terciio die Julii anno nono wupradicto inter horas septimani et octovani post meridiem eiusdem diei Edwardus Comes Oxon' et quidam Edwardus Baynam de civitate predicta taylor fuereunt insimules in quodam loco voca to le Backeyarde infra domum mansionalem Willelmi Cecyll militis apud St Clements Danes in comitatu predicto non intendent nec in animo habentes dampnum aliculus persone tunc et ibidem existenti. Et unusque eprum habems gladium de ferre et caliber vocatum foyles cum eisdem gladiis vocatis foyles alter eorum cum altero tunc et ibiden luserunt ad scientiam defenses. Ibid venit predictus Tomas Brinckenell ad locum predictum et idem Thomas tunc et ibidem ebrius existens et densus per oculis suis non habens set instigacione diabolics motus et seductus desperanter ipse incurrebat et cecidit super punctum predicti gladii vocati a foyle and valentem xyd quem predictus Edwardus Comes Oxon in manu sua dectra tunc et ibidem habuit et tenuit ea intercione ad ludendum [ut prefertur] Rove Cinus (?) prefatus Thomas cum eiodem gladio vocato foyle in antiore parte sui ipsuis sinistri femoris tunc et ibidem felonice seipsum percussit et pupugit et sibi ipsi dedit tunc et ibidem cum gladio predicto unam plagam mortalem profunditatis quaturo pollicia et latitudinis unius pollicii de qua quidem plaga mortuosa dictus Thomas tunc et ibidem instanter obijt et sic juratores predicti dicunt super sacrum suum quod predictus Thomas Brickenell' apud St Clements Danes predictam in comitatu predicto dicte vicesimo tercio die Julii anno supradicto modo et forma predictis felonice et voluntarie seipsum interfecit et occidit contra pacem dicte domine Regine coronam et dignitatem suas et sic idem Thomas Brickenell ad mortem suam devenit et non aliter neque aliquot alio modo quam ut superdictum est, in cuius rei testant tam predictus Coronarino quam Juratores predicti hinc inquisicionem sigilla sua alternate apposuerunt. Dat' die et anno primis supradictis

Per me Richardson Vale coronarium
fe(lo) de se

Thus we learn, evidently from the only witnesses to the slaying, the adolescent Earl of Oxford and the tailor Edward Baynam, that between the evening hours of 7 and 8 on 23 July 1567 (the

9th year of the Queen's reign) these two men were engaged in a sporting contest with fencing blades, called foils, in a place known as the Backyard, behind the house of William Cecil, knight, in the Strand, the parish of St Clements Danes in the "liberty" of Westminster. They played with the swords, practicing the science of defense, and had no (manifest) intention of hurting anybody "existing then and there." Suddenly a certain Thomas Brinknell, "yeoman," from the city of Westminster, arrived in the Backyard. (The inquest men gave no consideration to the fact that this Brinknell worked in the kitchen of Sir William Cecil and was therefore well known to the young Earl residing with the statesman.) The newcomer was drunk, the coroner reported, and his eyesight thick. Apparently "moved and seduced by devilish instigation" he flung himself blindly on the point of the foil which Edward de Vere held in his right hand. (The blade, by the way, was valued at eleven pence. But we are not told to whom it belonged. Nor was there any inquiry about the motivation of the miserable Tom in choosing the nobleman for his target when he might have attacked the tailor. None of the honest and law-fearing fellows at the inquest evinced a public curiosity about anything that transpired between the Earl and the underling that could have induced the latter to go against De Vere without a weapon on that hot day.) I have not the faintest notion, alas, of the meaning of "Rove Cinus." However it is clear that the Earl reacted to the undercook's attack by thrusting the sword he gript into the front of poor Tom's left thigh to a depth of four inches (literally "thumbs") one inch wide, and so fatally wounded the alleged assailant then and there. No surgeon seems to have been called; nor was a note made if any effort to stop the bleeding was undertaken by one of the witnesses. The coroner and his jurors determined that Brinknell had died by his own deed—felo de se.

They appear to have held the inquest on the same day, convening by candlelight, at the church of St Martins-in-the-

Fields, a short walk from Cecil House. There is a single name of prestige among the members of the jury that Richard Vale collected, surely at the request of Sir William Cecil. Randolph Holynshedd is better known to us as Raphael Holinshed, the renowned author of the *Chronicles of England, Scotland and Ireland*, which he later compiled for Cecil, and which the supreme dramatist cordially perused while writing his "Chronicle" plays. In the Brinknell manslaughter case the future composer of *Hamlet* found swift salvation, no rime or reason to sharpen his sarcasm against the insolence of office and the laws delay.

When William Cecil came to record his journal for July 1567 he remembered with painstaking clarity that "About the time" the undercook Thomas Brinknell was "hurt by the Earl of Oxford at Cecil House in the Strand," and that the coroner's inquest had reached the verdict of felo de se. A long time later, in June 1576, Cecil reminded his son-in-law in a letter lost: "I did my best to have the jury find the death of the poor man, whom he killed in my house, se defendendo." (Cecil Manuscripts at Hatfield, Calendar II, 170.) The statesman evidently considered the Backyard a part of his House. Today it is impossible to tell whether he deliberately misquoted the verdict of Richard Vale's jury in order to deliver a dose of wormwood.

By the dawn of Saint Patrick's day 1584 the dramatist had brooded and reflected enough on the destiny of poor Tom Brinknell to reach the peace and lucidity where he could handle the mystery of his manslaughter with the wit of the first scene of Act V in his most quoted tragedy. He brought two nameless Clowns on the stage, bearing spades to dig a grave, and had them commence a debate on the question "Is (one) to be buried in Christian burial that willfully seeks (his) own salvation?" The Second Clown's mind is religiously at rest because the State has instructed him, "the crowner hat sat on (the victim), and finds it Christian burial." His comrade in the ground wonders, "How can that be, unless (he killed himself) in (his) own defence?" But the Second Clown will not allow any intelligence to trouble the solidarity of church and state in his soul: "Why, 't is found so." The first buffoon then endeavors to solve the riddle in his solitary ear: "It must be 'se offendendo'; it cannot be else. For here lies the point: if I (slay) myself wittingly, it argues an act: and an act hath three branches; it is, to act, to do, and to perform: argal, (he slew himself) wittingly.

"Second Clown: Nay, but hear you, Goodman delver,—

First Clown: Give me leave. Here lies the water; good: here stands the man; good; if the man go to this water, and drown himself, it is, will he, nill he, he goes,—mark you that; but is the water come to him and drown him, he drowns not himself: aragal, he that is not guilty of his own death shortens not his own life.

Second Clown: But is this law?

First Clown: Ay, marry, I't; crowner's quest law."

In my belief we have here the confession of Edward de Vere, Earl of Oxford, that he was guilty of the abrupt death of Tom Brinknell; moreover, that he was responsible for shortening the life of Anne Cecil. He came to these conclusions by a road remote from coroner's inquest law, by the justice of the divine light in his head. But he could only endure the light by refracting it in his lone way, with laughter and various arts.

www.ingramcontent.com/pod-product-compliance
Ingram Content Group UK Ltd.
Pitfield, Milton Keynes, MK11 3LW, UK
UKHW040015200726
13854UKWH00001B/210

9 781450 211857